The Three Stages of Life

Passive
Active
Authoritative

By

Cheryl Salem

The Three Stages of Life
Passive Active and Authoritative

ISBN 978-1-890370-50-3

Printed in United States of America
Copyright © 2021 by Salem Family Ministries

Salem Family Ministries
PO Box 1595
Cathedral City, CA 92235
www.salemfamilyministries.org

Disclaimer: The views expressed in this book contain my personal opinions and experiences throughout my life and time spent in God's presence. I express them as my opinion and view only, and share them with you from my personal lifelong experience from my heart. I am only communicating what has worked for me personally, and what I have personally experienced with the Lord.

The Three Stages of Life 7

The Revelation of Light and Sound 15

Before Blood, During Blood, After Blood 33

The Circle of Threes 55

The Passive Stage 63

The Active Stage 71

The Authoritative Stage 79

The Third Day 93

Don't Look Back 101

Life Produces Life 115

Pay Attention to the Numbers 127

God's Shadow 141

God Revealed 145

Chapter One
The Three Stages of Life

In our society today much emphasis is put on youth. We are brainwashed into thinking that if we are not young (in years) then there is very little use for us anymore. We are told by so many sources, magazines, television, music, radio, and all social media platforms, once we have lost our *bloom* then productivity of life is over. As I have matured (that's a very nice, feminine way of saying that I am over 60,) I find that for the first time in my life, I have the wisdom to make the right choices, and skills to accomplish them, the mind to think and see them through, and the physical endurance to finish what I start.

Too often we are taught by the world we live in that our importance is over once we have reached a certain age. What a bunch of broccoli! We have been made to feel that if we don't do certain things while we are young then we will never accomplish anything.   As I have grown older, I am finding that I can't accept this way of thinking and for good reasons.

When I was younger, I didn't have the wisdom to do anything or say anything of any real importance and value. Now that I have some 'tried by fire' wisdom I refuse to throw it out and say, "Well, I didn't know this earlier when it would have mattered, and people would have listened."

NO! It matters now and we must learn to rethink what we thought. We must learn to see life in the eyes of truth and not through the minds of some immature human beings who have dictated to all of humanity the great value of youth and the throw away society of those who have finally the wisdom, the strength, and the forethought to go the distance.

What has happened to listening to those who have walked the road before us? What has happened to getting good advice from others of wise counsel? Where are our mentors who can help us not make the same mistakes of those who have gone before us? Because of our rebellious attitudes toward listening, understanding, and obeying advice of seasoned travelers on the road of life, we seem to continually fall in the same ruts, pits, and ditches of those who have traveled the road of life ahead of us. Like it or not, life circles back around over and over again. We can be like the children of Israel circling the Promised Land for forty years until we learn to respect and honor those who could help us go the distance.

We have opportunities to go around the road of life in a circle ever spiraling upward, continually changing, growing, and maturing. But because of our lack of advice, or our unwillingness to apply it, instead of gradually ascending on this precious road, we just go around and around on the same plane, never leaving the level in which we last traveled.

This leaves us continually making the same mistakes generation after generation. Instead of progressing forward and upward we begin to lose ground and begin to spiral into a pit of moral and spiritual decay.

Our minds, wills, and even physical bodies continue to look the same, or worse they progressively become weaker, sicker, and confused. We are a dirty, spotted, unwashed, and wrinkled cultural generation who has refused to take good counsel, always thinking that we are the smartest people in the room!

We have become so self-focused and self-centered that the word 'selfie' has been entered into the dictionary! We can change this direction but we must change our focus. We must take our eyes off of ourselves and put our eyes on King Jesus to begin the ever spiraling higher and higher spiritual journey.

Don't give up hope! There is a way to change, to get off of this merry-go-round (or should I say, sad-go-round), never progressing, never leaving the plane in which we find ourselves. There are ways to predict the future void of our past and the past of our ancestors. Our past does not have to predict our future, but to stop that cycle we must learn how to progress through the God given stages of life.

I am beginning to realize that the best way to get the wrinkles and spots out of our souls and spiritual lives is to live long enough to understand the purpose of this earth. A people without purpose and destiny are a people who will never move, never progress, and never ascend to new heights.

No matter how hard I tried to understand in my teens and twenties I just could not see the truth, because I did not have 'eyes to see.' With age our natural eyes may begin to dim but our spiritual eyes should become sharper and stronger. Oh, I thought that I was seeing and hearing truth. I thought that I was speaking and transforming others, but in reality, I was just the less blind leading the more blind. Thank God for grace, for only God can use us when we are unusable. He takes our efforts and turns them to success when there is no real reason or understanding with our actions. There are some things that can only come with tears and years. Harry says it best and I quote, "Knowledge comes through learning, but wisdom comes through living, and living the abundant life through Jesus Christ."

Now that I have more mature eyes to see what is happening I refuse to keep quiet and continue to perpetuate the lie that youth and plumpness of one's facial skin is what true joy and happiness is all about, when I know for sure that true joy, true happiness, true fulfillment of life can only come with the 'circles of life.'

I am not talking about the circles under the eyes that one gets from lack of sleep and rest. No, in fact, I am talking about the circles of life when finally we arrive at a place in life where we don't care what others think about us anymore. This is a place in life where our decisions are not based on what someone else might think or say, or what someone else might judge or criticize. This is a place called FREEDOM. Whom the Son sets free is free indeed. I am finally eternally free.

This is the most freeing place I have ever lived. This is a place where what others think of me means nothing to me; only what I think of myself means anything. Harry has said this our entire married life. "I must only be true to the face in the mirror. Without that I have nothing."

Talk about real freedom! For the first time in my life, I have the scars to prove that what I am saying is worth hearing, that the words that now flow from my mouth are not constantly being formed because this is what I think others want to hear. In fact, it is the exact opposite of that! I am free to be the woman God created and planned for me to be. I am free to teach, train, and hopefully inspire you to be the person God created and purposed you to be!

There is a river within me that has been forged with much hurt, pain, and tears and that river carries the words that flow out of my mouth. This river that flows from the very center of the 'tree of life', the very center of the garden of my life, is one that carries hope and healing for all to see and hear.

For the first time in my life, if no one wants to listen I could care less. Now I speak of the truths that I have learned and my heart's desire is to mentor and teach those whose heart is to learn the very essence of truth, the integral core existence of life itself, how to reach it, attain it, apply it to their lives, and begin to live it for all of eternity.

If no one wants to hear it, I don't care. I am not saying it any longer for approval or attention. I speak because I know for the first time in my life I finally have something to say. If anyone listens that is up to him or her. If anyone takes it to heart, that is up to them. My value is no longer based on other's opinions. My value is only based on what I know, not what I think.

What I know cannot be changed. It cannot be debated. It cannot be bent, or removed, or questioned. Light has penetrated my heart and there is not a force strong enough to remove it from me. Nothing can ever separate me from it. I choose it and it has chosen me.

What I write in this book is totally and completely freeing. It is not said because you must hear it, but because I must say it. Whether you apply and receive it is totally and completely up to you.

I really could care less any more. I am free from trying to impose what I believe on people I am free from trying to teach others how to live their lives. I am free from thinking that I am the only one who knows anything. I am free from the driving force that I must accomplish this or that so that I will be a success.

I am a success and I know it because I am happy. I am happy with my life. I am happy with my marriage. I am happy with my children. I am happy with my grandchildren. I am happy with what I get to do for the Lord. I am happy with my present and future life. I have chosen to forget my past. I am happy.

This happiness that I feel is not based on situations or circumstances. This happiness is not based on good things that have happened in my life. This happiness is not based on any earthly thing, except that I now know that I don't attain it. I can't earn it. I can't work hard enough to have it. I receive it. I possess it.   It is a free gift given to all of humanity who will only receive it!!!   Freedom is truly a choice, my choice, and ultimately for your life, your choice.

I grew up in Choctaw County Mississippi trying to achieve life to it's fullest. I thought that if I could reach my goals, overcome life's obstacles, run the race faster than anyone else that I would be free and happy. Wrong!!!!!!

Youth has only one view. It is not multifaceted, but very short sighted.   It thinks that it knows everything when it knows very little, if anything at all.

Youth thinks that wrinkles indicate the beginning of the end, when it actually indicates that life has just begun, the end of the beginning. Youth, it's not all that it's cracked up to be. I know.   I was young once and now I am not so young, but don't tell anybody, including me, because I will argue with you that youth can be renewed while waiting, and mine certainly has been.   My youth is renewed like the eagles.

As you read I hope that you will begin to see some of the truths that I have learned that have helped me make the transitions in life, not so much with grace, but with pizzazz and finesse.

Nothing in my life has ever come easy. It has always been a struggle, a fight, and a pushing, shoving, scratching, biting battle of my mind, will, and emotions.

There may be a few wrinkles in my face. I call them wisdom lines. Line upon line, precept upon precept. Isn't that how things are truly built that will last?   The lines on my face are just that, foundation lines upon which I have built a strong life in Christ.   These lines that etch my face are lines of a foundation that can never be shaken, never be brought down, and never be destroyed.

Each line has been earned.   Each scar that traces my face and body represents a place in the fire that has transformed me from who I thought I was supposed to be, into who I have become.

I have often thought about the scars on my face and body and even those emotional scars in my life.   I have often reflected on whether my 'eternal' body will have these scars.   I have often wondered whether the scars on my broken heart will be in my eternal spirit.

I think that not all scars are eternal, only those scars that have been deepened past the flesh level of life. How is that possible?

One day in prayer, I asked the Spirit of the Lord about the scars. I was reading my Bible and happened to be reading the passage where Jesus appeared to Thomas and the other disciples, after He had risen from the dead. He was in His glorified body when He presented Himself to them. In fact,

He walked right through the wall and appeared to them! They all believed it was Jesus but not Thomas. He doubted. Jesus simply asked Thomas to touch the scars in His hands to prove that He was who He said that He was. Thomas believed Jesus when He saw His scars in His eternal body.

I asked the Lord when I finished reading the passage, whether I would have the scars in my natural body in my eternal spirit body. He answered me, "You only get to keep the scars that change other people's lives."

When the scars of our lives have helped someone else, when they have changed the path of someone else's future, then we may keep them for eternity. No longer a scar but a star, a crown, maybe even a medal of a fight fought and won. I believe my scars are trophies, hopefully crowns that I may cast at His feet when I worship Him for eternity.

Chapter Two
The Revelation of Light and Sound

Have you ever thought about the very appearance of a circle? The definition is quite simple. A circle is defined in the Hebrew as:

Strong's OT: 2329

Chuwg —

1)   A circle, a circuit, a compass

2)   Brown-Driver-Briggs: the vault (of the heavens)

(From the Online Bible Thayer's Greek Lexicon and Brown Driver & Briggs Hebrew Lexicon, Copyright © 1993, Woodside Bible Fellowship, Ontario, Canada. Licensed from the Institute for Creation Research.)

By definition a circle is the vault of the heavens. When I think of a vault I think of a secure place to put my most important and valuable possessions. I have heard people say when someone tells them a secret that it is in the vault, implying that no one will be able to get it out of them! Then with that in mind could it be possible that humanity is God's most valuable and precious possessions since we are kept in God's circle?

When we think of our lives, as that precious to God then maybe it will make us put more value on our very existence and do something with the gift of life that has been given us.

Another definition of a circle is 'a circle, a circuit, a compass.' All are phrases that depict a never-ending movement, a continual movement of power and energy that passes from one location to another, round and round it goes. Of course, the very word, compass, gives us the idea that a circle is not about being lost (I've been going around in circles,) but that the circle of a compass is what actually helps direct our paths.

In the Book of Job we see a verse that talks about a circle that God draws.

"He drew a circular horizon on the face of the waters, at the boundary of light and darkness." Job 26:10 NKJV

God draws circles upon the earth. The circles of life make so much sense. The earth is round; it rotates on its axis. This circular movement is what gives us gravity to hold us on the earth.

The earth turns in a circular motion as it goes around the sun in a circular motion. The lesser light, the moon, circles the earth. Life on earth is not a flat plane. The earth is not flat, and men proved this many years ago. But somehow, we still tend to think horizontally and flat instead of vertically, round, and multidimensionally. We must change the way we think to change our direction. We must change our minds to change our futures. *"As a man thinks in his heart, so is he."* Proverbs 23:7. The way we think changes our direction, our paths, and the outcome and destiny in which we cross the finish line. How do you think? That's who you are.

In grade school we talk about the circle of food groups. In

science we talk about the circles of the existence of life. Even the Bible talks about the circular motion of the earth. In music we talk about the circle of 5ths. Every fifth interval moving upward or downward twelve moves will eventually bring one back to the first tone, a full circle.

"Do you not know? Have you not heard? Has it not been told you from the beginning? Have you not understood since the earth was founded? He sits enthroned above the circle of the earth." Isaiah 40:21-22 NIV.

Light and sound are circular. In fact, when you think about it, light is spherical and so is sound. Light goes in every direction from its source and so does sound. It is not just horizontal and vertical but also, every dimension, every degree, and in every direction.

Think of it this way. Imagine the tiniest ball of light and as it begins to shine forth it gets bigger and bigger in every possible direction to infinity. Sound is the same way in that it moves outward from the source of the sound in every degree, dimensional direction like a massive growing rippling wave into infinity.

Light and sound travel in every direction, up, down, front, back, and then every tiny place in between going up, down, back, and forward. Light and sound are waves. They emanate from the source outward, never ending right into infinity. Can you imagine every word you have ever said, every note you have ever sung is still 'sounding' further and further away from you creating a multidimensional path into eternity! Every word you ever said is still saying. Every prayer you have ever prayed is still praying. Every complaint you ever made is still complaining.

God is light. The Bible tells us so. That is why Einstein's theory of relativity is so important to us. Einstein proved that the only absolute in the entire universe is light. So he actually proved that the only absolute in the universe is God. God is Light. Just like a light wave, God's light is spherical, circular, and with every wave, ray, and frequency it has an infinite arrow, never ending in every direction.

Light and sound do not just move in circular and spherical directions, but each wave of light and sound are also, spherical and circular. Tones are round. There is a top, middle, and a bottom to every tone. That's why some people sing right on the pitch, while others sing on the top (sounding sharp) and others sing on the bottom of the tone (sounding flat.) Light and sound waves are not flat, but circularly dimensional, like a tube.

The studies of science and mathematics are so wonderful for us, because many times these realms of study prove God's Word. One of the greatest physicists of all time was Albert Einstein. His theory of relativity has been so powerful for our society.

Just in this one theory Einstein proved that God is the only absolute in the universe. By his studies and research, he proved that light couldn't be changed. It is constant and nothing can change it. God says in His Word, *"God is light."* I John 1:5. Furthermore God says, *"I am the Lord; I change not."* Malachi 3:6. Einstein proved through physics that God is absolute, and He cannot be changed.

Significant scientific discoveries for the church have emerged in the last few years. Over the past 100 years many discoveries about our human body have helped us understand our very existence and creation. But none has been more significant for me than scientists discovering the core of our human cells.

For years microscopes have been getting more and more

powerful. When they discovered the nucleus of the cell we were very impressed. Since then scientists discovered the center of the nucleus are the protons and neutrons, then the center of the protons and neutrons is the quark.

Quantum Wave Theory became the focus for us as worshipers, since it introduced the very center or core of human cells as sound waves. Quantum Wave Theory has been around since the early 1900s. Then around the turn of 2000 I became extremely interested after an extended vision from the Lord. I saw light slowed down to become sound! How did physicists discover this phenomenon that the Bible taught us from the very beginning?

God spoke us into existence! We were created out of the spoken sound of God! Now science is beginning to catch up to this one of many truths the Bible has always shown us. Scientists discovered that what they thought was the tiniest of our human existence was moving, wiggling, and vibrating in a petre dish. When they could identify what this movement was, this vibration within humanity, they discovered that the very core of our existence is a sound wave!

Deep inside, in the very core of our existence we are made up of a sound wave. God spoke humanity into existence and the sound of God is within every cell in your body! The Bible says that we *"wrestle not with flesh and blood, but (we wrestle) with principalities, powers, rulers of the darkness, spiritual wickedness in high places."* Ephesians 6:12. The word 'wrestle' in the Strong's concordance is defined as 'a vibration, to vibrate.'

The core in every cell of our human bodies is created to wrestle, to vibrate against powers, principalities, rulers of darkness, and spiritual wickedness in high places. We were not created to be defeated. We were created to take authority and dominion against the demonic dominions of this world.

The prince of this world is Satan and God has put within us, within the very core of all mankind, the ability to overcome the darkness, through our vibration of sound. Our wiggly cellular structure was designed by the Lord of hosts, to wrestle out of the grip, and release us from the stronghold of our enemy!

Doesn't that make you want to stop right now and start worshiping God with your vibrational cellular sound? Come on, stop and worship Him! He deserves it and you need to do it!

The millions and millions of cells that make up our human existence are actually millions and millions of warring, wrestling, vibrating sound waves! That explains why we are so easily affected by music. For years, I have heard that music is the universal language. Of course it is! We are made up of it! We can speak it! We can hear it! We can overcome with it!

One of the great discoveries since this one has been what was first hypothesized and then proven about the speed of light and sound. Scientists have now proven that when you slow a light wave down it essentially becomes sound, and when you speed a sound wave up it essentially becomes light. They have proven that light and sound run parallel to each other in every direction and there is a specific distance that creates the separation, but not even close to the same speed. Light and sound are separated by exactly forty octaves. Sound is forty octaves lower, and slower, than light. Light is forty octaves higher and faster than sound!

In ancient Hebrew the number 40 is defined as 'the end of testing and trials.' Consider the distance between light and sound as the end of testing and trials. Heaven is filled with light, not even one shadow is there. The earth is created out of sound. God spoke the entire earth's existence into being.

An octave is a musical measurement of eight different sequential tones. An octave is seven different notes, sounds, and frequencies plus the first one repeated at a full circle of sound. When the eighth one is added (eight is defined as 'new beginnings'), it is the first sound at a higher pitch, or wavelength. Don't hang up on that last statement. You know what an octave is; you just might not have known what to call it.

Do-Re-Mi-Fa-Sol-La-Ti-Do. That's an octave. Its eight sequential tones, notes, frequencies and in this pattern, it is ascending. The same is true when descending eight tones. Do-Ti-La-Sol-Fa-Mi-Re-Do. Go ahead and take a moment to prove you can sing by singing the eight-note scale.

You remember the movie 'The Sound of Music' right? Remember the lyrics that taught the whole world the scale of music? Do, a deer a female deer. Re, a drop of golden sun. Mi, a name I call myself. Fa, a long long way to run. Sol, a needle pulling thread. La, a note that follows Sol. Ti, a drink with jam and bread, and that brings us back to Do! These are the ascending tones of a musical scale. That's an octave. You did know what an octave is!

When going higher the eighth note is double the frequency or speed of the first pitch, therefore completing the circle of sound. One (Do), two (Re), three (Mi), four (Fa), five (Sol), six (La), seven (Ti), then eight (Do) is the same as the first one (Do), at a full circle of sound at a higher pitch. Thus, we have the circle of sound ever spiraling upward to a higher level, or ever spiraling downward to a lower level. (Do-Ti-La-Sol-Fa-Mi-Re-Do.)

Sound progresses in both directions, vertically and horizontally, circularly like the roots of a tree going down and the trunk going up! They are infinite in each direction.

Just because it gets too high or too low for us to hear with our natural ears, does not mean that it is not there or cannot be heard. Our ears can only hear within a certain low to high range of tones, but the sound is there regardless of whether you can hear it or not!

When you think about it in musical terms, using the musical alphabet it can become even clearer for you. Music has only seven letters. A, B, C, D, E, F, G. G is the seventh and last alphabet letter in the musical language. This is a progression of sound, spiraling upward or downward, but never going straight or horizontal.

Once the seventh sound is named, then the letters simply begin again with A, B, C, D, E, F, G, A, B, C, D, E, F, G, etc. An example of the frequency doubling is the frequency used to tune a piano. The measurement is A 440. That frequency A440 is what all instruments are tuned to so we can play together. When the octave is reached (A,B,C,D,E,F,G,A) the first A being the frequency tone of 440 then the second A is double in frequency at 880. These are the ascending notes. But you can also, reverse the tones to go lower and lower octave by octave.

Have you ever wondered why in the beginning of this world as we know it, the Bible says, *"In the beginning God created the heavens and the earth?"* Then the Bible goes on to say that, *"God said."* Why would God say anything? To whom was He talking? God is light. God is light and He is creating light, then why would He say or speak, *"Let there be light?"*

It is really quite simple when you think about it. God is moving at such tremendous speeds of light that to create light on our level, our slower lower level, God had to reduce the speed of light to create sound, forty octaves below the wave of 'light.' The realm of the spirit is based upon light. The realm of the earth is based upon sound. Humanity operates and moves at the speed of sound; the eternal realm operates and moves at the speed of light.

This explains why God said, *"Let there be light,"* in Genesis 1:3.   He is light, so to produce the earth, the flow of energy that is light in this lower and slower realm, light must be slowed down to produce earthly light (at a slower lower speed.)   Thus, sound becomes the end result and the power source of our earth's existence and the ultimate end result for humanity. Remember the core of our being; the core of our human cells is sound. This revelation makes it so powerful for us with our daily words, prayers, and confessions. *"Death and life are in the power of the tongue: and they that love it shall eat the fruit thereof."* Proverbs 18:21KJV.

What we say has power. We have power to speak life. We have power to speak death. Whichever power we release upon the earth, whether death or life, we will eat the fruit of what we have spoken. I choose to speak life.

The purpose of the earth is to reproduce the light of God at a slower rate of motion for humanity. Everything is in motion in the universe. Sound, the spoken word, music, noise, everything is a slowed down version of God to the earth when we are speaking life. Time is not necessary in the dimension where God is present. Past, present, and future are joined together without the necessity of time. But the earth is a time of testing and trials for us. (Remember, we exist forty octaves lower and slower than light.) The earth is our womb experience producing our eternal being. The earth is the womb of heaven. Who we develop into while here on earth is who we will be birthed into eternity as an eternal being. It is our time to make a choice. Who will we choose to serve? Who will we choose to love?   Who will we choose to become?   Whose image will we choose to reflect?   The earth is all about choice, my choice, and your choice. God is giving us a choice to love Him, to serve Him, to be 'one' with Him.   Before time began, we were already in God, but not by choice, only by design.   God took us out of Him, and slowed us down enough to give us 'time to choose' Him.

Life is a journey filled with many choices. We have been given power here to make the right choices for our future, to fulfill God's plan and purpose for our destinies. Choose wisely. Your future self will thank you.

Light moves at such a fast rate that with our human abilities we cannot measure it within ourselves. For us to understand the speed of light, it is as if time does not exist to the speed of light. It does, but it is beyond our comprehension of measurement.   Time is our friend, not our enemy.   Time is what allows us to develop our relationship with God, giving us the time to learn to trust Him.   In this realm of time and space we actually experience a moment with God in an aspect of years.

Time is for our comprehension. When God speaks by revelation to humanity, we must have the dimension of time here on the earth so we can process the layers, the dimensions, and the depth and bring it to the surface of our thinking, one layer at a time.

Meditate on the Word day and night. Why do we need to do this? When we meditate we slow down a thought even more so we can separate the layers of thoughts and comprehend and receive them. This is what I believe is truly revelation from the dimension of the spirit to the dimension of the mind.

A day and a night comprises the full circle of the moon, a light source, around the earth. A year is the full circle of the earth around the sun, a light source. God is teaching us to circle, to move, to go forward, which is not really forward, but circular, ever spiraling upward like a whirlwind if we could actually move that fast. The circle of sound in music is a perfect way to imagine it. We circle the clock by the minute, the hour, and the day. We circle the year through twelve months of the calendar. It's time worshipers, to 'circle up.'

What else is circular that is continually referenced throughout the Bible? What about trees? The trunk is not only circular, but also, vertical. From Genesis to Revelation there are hundreds and hundreds of references to trees, most of which are made in relationship to mankind.

Starting in the Garden of Eden in Genesis 2:9 there are dueling trees or maybe we should call them balancing trees. For how can you truly know what is light without dark? How can we know what is cold without hot?   How can we know what is good without evil?   How can we know what is up without down? How can we know what is inside without outside?   Should I go on? This is truly the balance of our universe.

For everything there is an opposite. For every action there is a reaction. For male there is female, his other sight, his other side, his other view (Ancient Hebrew definition of the word helpmate.) For night there is day. For land there is sea.   For good there is evil. For blessing there is curse. For life there is death.

Everything is most easily identified when the exact opposite is revealed. Then how could we have ever been able to understand the true love of God without the intense hate of Satan for humanity?

This explains why Satan was in the Garden in the first place. This explains why Satan, as fallen Lucifer was thrown 'like lightning' to the earth. Jesus said in Luke 10:18 that He saw Satan fall like lightning to the earth. There was a whole universe out there. Why did he have to fall on our planet? The earth is the third planet from the sun. This is the planet for the bride of Christ to be developed in the womb of the earth. Satan had to be thrown down here.

Mankind took fallen Lucifer's place as the third archangel position under the authority of the Holy Spirit. (This is too big a revelation to just slide it through the text here. We will discuss further in another book.)

Satan was placed here on the earth by God so mankind, the two Adams as Genesis 5:1 so aptly puts it, could be able to identify the goodness of God and not take for granted the love of God that was and still is given so freely and abundantly! Can we fully understand the love of God without being subjected to the hate of our worst enemy, fallen Lucifer, now Satan?

"And the LORD God made all kinds of trees grow out of the ground--trees that were pleasing to the eye and good for food. In the middle of the garden were the tree of life and the tree of the knowledge of good and evil." Genesis 2:9 NIV.

Two trees, one is good and filled with life. The other tree is not good, no wisdom, only knowledge of good and evil. The tree in itself, like knowledge, is neither good nor bad. It is what humanity decides to do with it and creates the evil from the heart of mankind. It is what grows down and up, roots and branches that create the outcome, whether good or evil.

In the NIV translation the word 'trees' is referenced 137 times. The word 'tree' is referenced 180 times in the NIV and the phrase 'tree of life' is referenced 11 times. In the King James Version 'trees' is referenced 157 times, 'tree' is referenced 205 times, and 'tree of life' is referenced 10 times.

In the first chapter of the Psalms the parallel is made between mankind and trees. Many references make the comparison! *"The trees of the field shall clap their hands,"* Isaiah 55:12 is a wonderful depiction of nature and mankind worshiping the Lord in parallel.

"Blessed is the man who does not walk in the counsel of the wicked or stand in the way of sinners or sit in the seat of mockers. But his delight is in the law of the LORD, and on his law, he meditates day and night. He is like a tree planted by streams of water, which yields its fruit in season and whose leaf does not wither. Whatever he does prospers."
Psalm 1:1-3 NIV

The continual reference to humanity as 'trees' throughout the text, the trunk of a tree being circular, and the references throughout this book that will lead us to an upward spiral traveling toward a destiny somewhere beyond the level where we are today is ever pointing us toward a journey. Life is filled with levels, stages, progression, ever moving onward, forward, and upward!

How can you tell the age of a tree? You can't without getting inside of its trunk. Once inside you count the circles, the circles of life, inside the tree trunk, which gives you the age, the years the tree has been on the earth. You can't really tell how 'old' a person is either without getting inside of them. Age is not a number, age is a destination of maturity, which can only be reached by pressing, pushing, resisting, and growing. Life is not killed in the fires of trial and tribulations; life is birthed out of the fires we endure, to come out of the fire purified, tried, and tested.

Life is a journey, but I propose to you that the journey is not horizontal as so many of us have thought for centuries, but rather it is a vertical journey beyond any place in the heavenlies where mankind has managed to go through a spaceship or even a telescope.

This place so far beyond our earthly abilities to travel is not only attainable but is a total and complete part of God's plan for our destinies. This destiny designed and made possible by our loving Father God, for us solely because we are humans, mankind, and He loves us! He has called us to fulfill the greatness within us.

It is our natural tendency to think horizontally. We think left to right, the beginning and the end, A to Z, Alpha to Omega. We think from when we were born to when we die as a straight line across the earth, horizontally traveling through time. But I believe that the all-powerful God of the universe created us to circularly move, not horizontally, but circularly, ever traveling slowly upward, spiraling toward the heavens, and our eternal destiny.

When Elijah was translated from earth to eternity, without dying by the way, the Bible passage says that he 'went up' in a whirlwind in a chariot of fire. A whirlwind makes a very fast circular upward motion. I believe that throughout our lives God sends us chariots that can transport us from the place that we are to the next level, next layer, next position that is destined and ordained for God's people. One thing that I am absolutely sure of, our destiny, is 'up' from where we are right now. So don't look down, and don't look back. Look up, your future is upon you!

Every situation in which you have ever found yourself can be the chariot ride that God has sent for you to transport you upward toward eternity, ever circling the Tree of Life, our very life source, the light of whom we truly are. Or we can see each trial and tribulation, each circumstance and situation as a crushing and devastating enemy attack sent to kill, steal, and destroy.

One thing is for sure; I don't despise anything that I have come through. Each and every place I have found myself in life has been the stepping-stone, the building block, and even in some situations, the sling shot that propelled me upward toward the destiny that God has designed for me. Like Joseph, toward the end of his life, he would not blame his brothers for throwing him into a pit and selling him into slavery. He simply said it was God's plan and destiny to get him to the end result, and fulfillment to save nations of people and his own family.

For us to *'ride upon the high places of the earth'* as Deuteronomy 32 so aptly puts it, we must learn to not lie down under the image of the devastating enemy attacks that we feel we are experiencing. Rather we need to learn to recognize God's chariots sent to bring us up 'hither', to the higher places to be seated with Christ that is so eloquently written of in the Book of Ephesians 2:6. I am already seated in heavenly places. My head is in heaven; my feet are in time.

In my life I have had many encounters with God's presence. Many times, in dreams God has revealed His divine protective 'hiding place' for me. As a child when I felt like my life was out of control, or for whatever reason I was worried or stressed in my mind, I would always go to sleep thinking about my God, my strength. And many times, night after night, I would dream of flying at very fast speeds, never afraid, never nervous.

I always felt that I was just out of reach of harm, that nothing could touch me no matter how hard the unseen shadowy figure of the enemy tried. The enemy could not touch me, nor could any demonic and dark hand grasp my feet as they dangled down in my flight position. Even when I have had visions of God in my adult life, sometimes dreams, and then other times outright visions and revelations of God appearing to me, each time God, the Father, showed me incredible things that took me months of meditation to get 'slowed down enough' for the 'light of His presence' moves at such tremendous speeds and while I am with Him, I completely understand. It is only when I try to slow down the revelations of God's supernatural presence, the light of God, to the level and speed of sound, trying to express in words, in earthly terms, what was imparted to me in a flash of revelation, that I find myself extremely frustrated. Because what is expressed in only moments with Father God takes months and months to express in our dimension of time and space.

Each time I have been with God I knew that I was being transported in something. It was exhilarating, fun, and totally without fear. Now I realize that through the trials and troubles of life that I have experienced, each and every time, God sent His chariot to take me up, "Climb in," I can just hear the Spirit driver saying, "so that you can soar with the eagles."

When an eagle is making an assent in flight he circles upward. He never goes straight up, but rather circles, and circles until he reaches the jet stream that he needs to move to his next destination.

I now believe that Elijah was so in tune with the Spirit of God here on the earth, that with each and every trial that he experienced, God continued to send His chariot. One of those chariot journeys took Elijah to such great heights in God that he just didn't come back.

We have another account of this happening with Enoch in Genesis. The Bible says that Enoch walked in habitual fellowship with God. And when giving the history of his life, the Bible says, "Enoch was no more." There is no record or account that he ever died. They never found a body. He just left the earth.   When we walk with God we walk and live and breathe and exist in this earth at a different dimension than other people. Many people would like to be in this place, but they are not willing to go through what it takes to get to this place.

God's presence is so intense that flesh cannot survive there. Only those who have totally and completely purified themselves, cleansed themselves with the washing of the water, and passed through the fire. Only those, whose earthly life means nothing except to obey God, can withstand the intenseness of His presence.

It is only in our interior, totally disconnected with our exterior person, that we can withstand the intense fire of God's presence.   God longs to purify us, to cleans us from unrighteousness.   So much so that He sacrificed His only Son, so that we can have a better way, a new law, a law that supersedes and does away with the law that is in existence because of the choice of mankind through Adam.   The law of sin and death that became legalized because of the choice of Adam could not be undone. But rather, there had to be a better law, a higher law written. This law had to give God's people a way of escape, a way to defend themselves against the previous law.

This law is the undeniable sacrifice of Jesus, God's only Son, and the pure Lamb of glory, without spot or wrinkle.   Jesus is the Word, the written Word.   In the Book of John, the Bible says that *"In the beginning was the Word . . . and the Word became flesh and dwelt among us."* God wrote this new law, the new way of escape from the very beginning. That is why the Bible says that *'In the Beginning was the WORD.'*

Jesus was already the new law, even before Adam fell, and the law of sin and death were introduced. Jesus was already the existence of a written way, a written law, and a written escape plan for all of God's people. By this ultimate sacrifice, we now have a better choice, a way of escape, and a way of defense for all time. The old law of sin and death could not be undone, so there had to be written another law, that if accepted could give life forevermore for anyone who would receive this free gift of God.

A plan, a journey for mankind, was set in motion. Levels, layers, and destiny became the pathway for each of us to walk. We can choose to walk with Him and fulfill each word already written in our Book of Life, or we can pick up our own pen and start rewriting and editing the plan of the Lord.

I don't know about you, but I believe, the One who has already been with me in my future, actually knows the better way for me. Since Jesus plainly told us that He is the way, I think I'll listen to the GPS voice of the One who created me and already has a powerful plan for me to fulfill completely written and published in my very own Book of Life. How about you? Are you about finished editing and rewriting what God has written for you?   It's about time.

Chapter Three
Before Blood, During Blood, After Blood

I have been able to identify through my prayer and revelation three stages, or levels, of our life's journey here on earth. You could call them phases, even seasons. Each phase has other phases inside of them, like our cells. Each season seems to have smaller seasons within them. Let's talk about a very obvious progression of life within a woman's journey.

Before blood
During blood
After blood

Even though in a woman's life cycle these stages are very visible, a man goes through the same three stages. Jesus went through these three stages and we will discuss them.

Now don't get all hung up on these next few pages and scripture as I believe it is necessary to have the revelation of your own life's natural and supernatural journey through each stage. Each one is to be celebrated and enjoyed to the fullest. Don't shut down over the biology. I have something much deeper for you to see and realize but it's much easier to see the deeper things once you realize the simplicity of it.

We all know that a woman goes through these three stages of life. She is a little girl and hasn't started her period yet. This is the 'before blood' stage. Then she reaches an age where her body begins to produce an egg each month from her ovaries and thus the 'during blood' stage is entered. Once she is no longer productive in giving birth to children, the eggs stop producing, the womb dries up, and the blood stops 'after blood'. This circle of life in a female's body is very easy to see and understand.

Let's apply it to scripture and see some specific numbers associated with a female baby's life and then in comparison, with a male baby's life. There are always things to learn from numbers. When reading your Bible, don't miss the numbers or the meaning associated with the numbers. Let the Word speak to you in every layer. Everything in the Word of God is important, every jot and tittle, so consequently, every number has deep and profound significance when allowing the revelation of God's Word in your heart and mind.

There is an interesting scripture depicting what happens for a woman, a mother, once she has given birth. The birthing of both the male and the female had a purification process for the mother during the times of the Law of Moses. Each was unique and different, depending on whether a male or a female child.

In the ancient Hebrew language 'mother' is defined as 'strong water.' It takes water for certain levels of purification. The Word of God is referred to as the water of the Word many times throughout the scriptures. It takes the washing of the water of the Word to purify and cleanse us and make us ready and presentable to stand before our King.

In this purification process the baby's only part to play in this happened on the 8th day for the male child. This was the ritual act of circumcision, the cutting of the foreskin, the dead unproductive flesh. The first covenant between man and God is in this act of obedience. For the female it is also a type of circumcision over time in the second stage of life. Through the process of time, and the journey of life, the female will shed unproductive dead flesh from her womb each month.

A female's circumcision is a sign and a wonder passed down from one generation of female to the next generation of female. God uses the female to show the ongoing, forever, blood covenant He has made with humanity through the motherhood of every female. As she bleeds in the menstrual cycle each and every month once she has entered the active stage of her physical body, she becomes an eternal sign of God's blood covenant. Since we are spirit, soul, and body we must enter into the three stages of life in each and every part of who we are. We are triune, entering into covenant with a triune God.

Let's look at the scripture below paying close attention to the numbers presented for the male and female babies.

*"The LORD said to Moses, 'Say to the Israelites: A woman who becomes pregnant and gives birth to a son will be ceremonially unclean for seven days, just as she is unclean during her monthly period. On the **eighth** day the boy is to be circumcised. Then the woman must wait **thirty-three** days to be purified from her bleeding. She must not touch anything sacred or go to the sanctuary until the days of her purification are over. If she gives birth to a daughter, for **fourteen** days the woman will be unclean, as during her period. Then she must wait **sixty-six** days to be purified from her bleeding. When the days of her purification for a*

son or daughter are over, she is to bring to the priest at the entrance to the Tent of Meeting a year-old lamb for a burnt offering and a young pigeon or a dove for a sin offering.

He shall offer them before the LORD to make atonement for her, and then she will be ceremonially clean from her flow of blood. These are the regulations for the woman who gives birth to a boy or a girl. If she cannot afford a lamb, she is to bring two doves or two young pigeons, one for a burnt offering and the other for a sin offering. In this way the priest will make atonement for her, and she will be clean.'" Leviticus 12:1-8 NIV.

The mother's waiting period to be presented as clean for her female baby is double the days for her male baby. The male waiting period is easier to understand when we recognize the 8th day is for circumcision of the male.

The female has a personal and private circumcision that happens when she transitions from the first stage of her life (no blood) to the second stage of her life (during blood.) The female body begins to produce life through ovulation in the second (during blood) stage of her life. The female has two types of circumcision. The first one is with the Lord for purification when she begins to bleed through menstruation. Her egg drops on the 14th day of her cycle (circle of life) which correlates with the scripture given for a female baby, 14 days.

Then fourteen days later if she has not become pregnant her body produces a type of circumcision through the removal of the inner wall of the uterus. A young woman enters into her purification and production stage of life through this 'blood stage.' She has a sign of God's eternal covenant through her natural body each and every month. Menstruation is not a curse! It is a divine sign of covenant between God and His daughters for the blood stage of her life.

Then when a female decides to marry, and she has sex with her husband there is yet another circumcision when the female hymen is broken, and she takes a blood covenant with her husband from the fulfillment of their physical covenant. That's why premarital sex can be so destructive. It's a blood covenant that produces soul ties. Everything we assume as being "natural" affects our soul and spirits eternally.

God loves women. He uses females from generation to generation to be a sign of an eternal blood covenant between God and humanity. He created the feminine body to bleed when sexual covenant is made with her husband. A divine soul connection is made at that point and through the blood oneness is attained. Thus, the scripture that states, two become one, is in reference to this divine blood covenant between man and woman. Life (of the marriage) is in the blood.

We can see the cycle of a woman's covenant in a circular motion, as the earth turns and a month passes, then the power of reproduction begins again, and another opportunity comes to produce a life. If this doesn't happen, then the cleansing circumcision process begins again.

Circular . . . each and every turning of the earth represents another pattern of movement in a circular motion. The continual monthly circles of bleeding in a woman's body, is a sign to us that the covenant of Jesus' shed blood goes on and on forever. Cleansing is eternal, not temporal. It is heavenly not earthly. The devil has lied to women for generations trying to make us accept that menstruation is our 'curse' to bear. Nothing could be further from the truth. God so adores and loves women that He trusts us to carry the blood covenant within our bodies from generation to generation.

Many women would say that they have pain with the

monthly bleeding. Many think it is a repercussion of the curse. Nothing could be further from the truth. It is a covenant sign of the power of our human circumcision both male and female with our Lord, creating a pathway for righteousness for humanity. When the male is circumcised it comes with a level of discomfort, yes, even pain. Covenant costs us. We would never pay the pain price that the Father God paid when He gave His only Son to pay the price for us. His pain was beyond our human comprehension. So, suck it up and move on with life. Pain is a part of the journey. We aren't home yet. Speak to your body and command it to line up with the Word of God. You have been chosen to carry the covenant sign of Almighty God within you.

This is just a reminder, a sign, to us that the pain that Jesus suffered was the eternal covenant that never ends, connecting the human slowed down sound wave, to the parallel heavenly light wave that is higher and above us. Because the bleeding is a process for the female, each and every month, it reminds us that our purification throughout our lifetime is also, a process. Remember, we can't embrace the promise and ignore the process. There is always a journey connected to a destiny.

The process is the element of time that is given to us on the earth to help us. This giving of time to us helps us make correct choices. Time is our friend, not our enemy. Time helps us see things correctly and clearly. Time is the slowed down process in which a light wave becomes a sound wave. The slowing down in frequencies, forty octaves, to be exact, makes us understand that our lives here on earth are a process. We must not get impatient and give up. We must press forward, never look back, and continue on toward the promise of God for our lives and our futures.

The three stages, before blood, during blood, and after blood are much easier to see in a woman's life (the feminine side of the trinity of God) because a woman starts to bleed, bleeds, and then stops bleeding in her lifespan. But it must also, be represented in a male's life because of the scripture in the beginning of this chapter and the reference to blood that relates to the male gender. God loves humanity, both male and female. He makes covenant with us when we allow it and accept it.

In the scripture verses the numbers 7, 8, and 33 correlates with the male's life. The mother of the male is unclean for 7 days. The #7 is God's divine, complete, and perfect number. It is one full circle of a week. The male child is circumcised on the 8th day. The number '8' means new beginnings.

This is a fresh clean start for the male child; covenant has been cut and all things are new, fresh, and clean again. This is a cutting of flesh and blood is shed. With every male child a new generation can begin without any curses from the former generation.

There is then the period of purification for 33 days that must be done by the mother. These 33 days are for purification for her, a setting apart, until the process is fulfilled. Jesus' life on the earth was for a span of 33 years. Jesus was set apart to bring purification for all mankind. The mother represents the third position of the Godhead, through the Holy Spirit as He came alongside Jesus to help Him during His 33 years of life here on earth.

For the female the numbers '14' and '66' correlate with the purification process for every female's life. For a period of two weeks (14 days), double the time of the male, the mother is ceremonially unclean. Once a young lady enters her 'during blood' stage of life, the number fourteen will become a part of her daily experience. On the 14th day of each month her egg will drop, and then if she is not impregnated during her ovulation, another 14 days later she will have a supernatural circumcision of her womb and the inner lining of dead unproductive flesh will be purified from her body. Physically the mother bleeds as if she is having a monthly period after giving birth. She is considered ritually unclean while she is bleeding. This is also, a physical time of purifying her body.

Then there is no circumcision for the female as a baby. This circumcision comes later with the Lord when she begins her monthly menstruation and with a man/husband when the hymen is broken, the cutting of covenant with her counterpart, her other sight, her other side, her other view, the male, that she will become one for all of eternity.

Since, when the choice of oneness is attained spiritually and physically with the breaking of the hymen, blood is shed, and the oneness covenant is cut, there is no need for the female to be circumcised at birth because in God's sight she and He are one through the mother's blood until the female baby grows and enters her own personal blood covenant with Him. She will bleed as a sign of covenant with the Lord for all her reproductive blood stage of life.

By the bleeding of the hymen when male and female make eternal covenant, this in turn joins the female not just to the male, but also, to his heritage, his genealogy, and to his covenant with his God. There is the period of purification, a setting apart, for the female for 66 days, once again, double the time for the male counterpart. The female's setting apart of 66 days is a sign of the Word of God fulfilling our purification process through the washing of the water of the Word of God since there are 66 books of the Bible.

The female should never feel less than the male. If anything, these numbers represent the doubling of all things for the female. It also, should make very clear to us that God's plan is for male and female to become one by choice, thus the circumcision of the male at the 8th day and then the breaking of the hymen through the choice made to become one, shows us that God sees husband and wife as 'one flesh.' No longer are they two, but 'one' by choice in His Sight.

Since time is irrelevant for God, He is past, present, and future, at the same 'time,' this act of circumcision and monthly bleeding is an eternal sign to us that God sees us, male and female in our original state, two sides, two voices, two opinions, joined through blood covenant as one body.

When you think of male and female in the terms of sound you can see that the female (14) is the double of the male (7). In the terms of sound waves in music, pitch goes higher with each doubling. The woman's voice is one octave higher generally than a male's voice.

When the male goes into puberty, and steps into the active portion of his life, his voice, and his pitch drops one octave. Thus, the female is represented in a doubling of pitch above the male. The male is the foundation upon which the female goes up higher! In a later chapter we will discover a greater dimension and the deep truths about the number 14.

Jesus lived on this earth in a flesh body for 33 years. Jesus represents the male gender of humanity. His Word represents the female gender. Humanity is made in the image of the triune Godhead, Father, Son, and Holy Ghost. For this image to be complete on the earth then there must be triune represented, a connection between earth and heaven must be established.

It has been suggested time and time again that Jesus needed a female counterpart on the earth. This is not necessary, because He already had a female counterpart, not a flesh one, but an eternal Spirit One. There is a female side of God in the triune Godhead and we will prove it throughout these next few pages.

The number of the books of the Bible is 66 books. The Word of God, the Bible, represents the female gender of humanity. Of course, that would be obvious that 'Word' would be women! Women love words, love to communicate, etc. What a revelation! The Bible is, according to the Book of John, the Word of God. It is evident that the Word came with Jesus, for John says, *"In the beginning was the Word, and the Word became flesh and dwelt among us."* Jesus is the Word and the Word is Jesus.   They are one.

But don't miss the other feminine side of the Godhead through the Holy Spirit. Jesus described the Holy Spirit in John 14 as our helpmate! Helpmate is the term given by God for the female side of humanity! The definition of helpmate in ancient Hebrew is, 'His other side, his other sight, his other view.'

Timing is everything in God. There is nothing on this earth that is by coincidence. All happens here by ultimate design, and yet, we are given total freedom of choice to choose our fate for all eternity. The irony is that our God is an all knowing, all seeing, God. He not only knows and sees past, present, and future all at the same time, but it all happens at the same time IN HIM!

This can only be fathomed by our finite minds when we think of God, the earth, and all time and humanity, from a vertical position, like the trunk of a tree ever spiraling upward toward eternity.

God

Past   Present   Future

Vertical   Horizontal   Circular

From God's upper position, above the earth, He can see everything and be everywhere all at the same time. *"In the beginning was the Word, and the Word was with God, and the Word was God. The same was in the beginning with God."* John 1:1-2 KJV.

Notice that the scripture says that the Word, which is obviously Jesus, was in the beginning with God. It is beyond our natural ability to think in a vertical position so we must go into our soul, our spirit man, to think beyond the natural human progression of things.

We know from all teachings of creation that the female came after the male. I propose to you a slight adjustment in that thinking. I don't believe that the female was created after the male. It is not scripturally correct to think that way. I believe the male and the female were created in the same body in the beginning at the same time, and then separated/divided later.

"And God said, 'Let Us make man in Our image, after Our likeness: and let them have dominion over the fish of the sea, and over the fowl of the air, and over the cattle, and over all the earth, and over every creeping thing that creepeth upon the earth.' So God created man in His own image, in the image of God created He him; male and female created He them." Genesis 1:26-27 KJV.

Here we can see that both male and female were created. If this is true and those of us who believe that the Bible is infallible, even if I cannot imagine it, we can see that in the beginning there were both male and female. How is this possible when the female version does not show up (in our minds) until God puts Adam to sleep and creates woman? Or did He?

Let's look at this same verse in the Amplified Classic

translation and see a clearer picture of the true meaning of this verse. *"God said, Let Us [Father, Son, and Holy Spirit] make **mankind** in Our image, after Our likeness, and let **them** have complete authority over the fish of the sea, the birds of the air, the [tame] beast, and over all of the earth, and over everything that creeps upon the earth."* Genesis 1:26.

It is much easier to see in this version that God made mankind, not just the male half of mankind. He gave THEM complete authority, not just 'him' authority. Eve was not an afterthought! Eve was named Adam in the beginning and she was given dominion and authority just as the male half of mankind was given dominion and authority. They only needed one name, because they were in one body. He named them both Adam. (Genesis 5:1)

Now let's go on to see when God divided mankind like He had already divided everything else He had created. He created and divided light from dark. He created and divided day from night. He created and divided land from sea. Shall I go on? He simply created mankind, and then He did the next step. He divided them from one body into two bodies.

*"And the LORD God said, 'It is not good that the man should be **alone**; I will make him a help meet for him.'"* Genesis 2:18 KJV.

In the Strong's Hebrew definitions the word alone means: OT: 905 Bad (bad); from OT: 909; properly, separation; by implication, a part of the body, **branch of a tree**, bar for carrying; figuratively, chief of a city; especially (with prepositional prefix) as an adverb, apart, only, besides:

KJV - alone, apart, bar, besides, branch, by self, **of each alike**, except, only, part, staff, strength.

(Biblesoft's New Exhaustive Strong's Numbers and Concordance with Expanded Greek-Hebrew Dictionary. Copyright (c) 1994, Biblesoft and International Bible Translators, Inc.)

Notice two phrases, 'branch of a tree' and 'of each alike.'

"I am the true vine, and My Father is the vinedresser. Every branch in Me that does not bear fruit He takes away; and every branch that bears fruit He prunes, that it may bear more fruit. You are already clean because of the word, which I have spoken to you. Abide in Me, and I in you. As the branch cannot bear fruit of itself, unless it abides in the vine, neither can you, unless you abide in Me. **I am the vine, you are the branches.** *He who abides in Me, and I in him, bears much fruit; for without Me you can do nothing. If anyone does not abide in Me, he is cast out as a branch and is withered; and they gather them and throw them into the fire, and they are burned. If you abide in Me, and My words abide in you, you will ask what you desire, and it shall be done for you. By this My Father is glorified, that you bear much fruit; so you will be My disciples."* John 15:1-8 NKJV

I propose that when God made 'man' that He made both the male and the female in one body, in one flesh, because that would be 'in His image,' three in One in unity. All three of the Godhead made mankind.

"This is the Book of the generations of Adam. In the day that God created man, in the likeness of God made He him; male and female created He them; and blessed them, and called their name Adam, in the day when they were created." Genesis 5:1-2 KJV.

This scripture proves that male and female were first created at the same time in the same body and named one name. Later on, God puts Adam (both male and female) to sleep and does the separation of each side, making both a male and a formed female body. Obviously, the male counterpart continued to keep the original body and the female received the second body with maybe some adjustments to the 'models' to make sure they fit together physically once reunited in covenant.

The power that can be attained with the 'chosen' union of male and female is almost beyond our sphere of comprehension. This earth is created to give mankind a choice, a choice to operate as one, in unity, a choice to love God and, once again, become one with God Almighty.

I propose to you the sole purpose of the earth is to give mankind a choice to love God, to be 'one' with God, thus the reason for creation. We were all in God before the earth was created, not by choice but by design. I propose to you that 'by design' was not good enough for our God. His desire for us is to not be 'IN HIM' by design but for us to be 'IN HIM' by our own choice!

Just as His desire for us is to choose to be 'one' with Him, therein, lies the power of ONENESS. In our choosing to die to self and become 'one' with HIM, ultimate power and authority is attained. It must also apply to HIS IMAGE . . . humanity, mankind. When we were created both male and female in one body it was by design that we were one, unified. In this is no power. Oneness by itself does not create power.

Power is only attained through our choices, choosing to be one, to walk as one, dying to our own desires, our own will, our own flesh, to become ONE by choice, not by design, herein lies the power, the complete authority that must be attained for God to be seen on the earth!

As I read with revelation eyes, I see that male and female

were in one body and God said that this is not good. There is no power in one by design. There must be a choice to walk as one, operate as one, and truly be one. So, God put the male/female human to sleep and God pulled the female side out of the fire of humanity, thus creating 'his other side.' Now the creation of mankind is upon the earth, divinely separated, with the choice to operate, act, and become ONE.

*"And Adam gave names to all cattle, and to the fowl of the air, and to every beast of the field; but for Adam there was not found a **help meet** for him. And the LORD God caused a deep sleep to fall upon Adam and he slept: and He took one of his ribs, and closed up the flesh instead thereof."* Genesis 2:20-21 KJV.

In the ancient Hebrew the word male means 'his hand is in the midst of the fire.' The female means 'what comes out of the fire.' You can see just by these definitions that the female came out of the fire, not out of the rib of the male. She came out of the fire of mankind. The 'fire' in this instance is actually what the union, or unity of both male and female in complete agreement creates.

God said, "I AM an all-consuming fire." So, when male and female were in one body, the fire of God was present. The female was taken from the fire of mankind where the hand is at his side. The female was not created to be under man's feet, rather at his side from whence she came. What comes out of the fire? (female) His hand is in the midst of the fire. (male)

"And the rib, which the LORD God had taken from man, made He a woman, and brought her unto the man." Genesis 2:22 KJV.

Notice that the woman did not have to be created, just fashioned, formed, and made. Why? Because she had already been created. This process merely meant forming a new body of one becoming two by design, so that a future choice could be made for two to become one.

"And Adam said, this is now bone of my bones, and flesh of my flesh: she shall be called Woman, because she was taken out of Man. Therefore shall a man leave his father and his mother, and shall cleave unto his wife: and they shall be one flesh. And they were both naked, the man and his wife, and were not ashamed." Genesis 2:23-25 KJV.

Notice that the male and the female were created in the beginning and that 'they, ' not 'he' or 'she,' but 'they' were given **complete authority.**

The words 'help meet' or 'help mate' has a revealing definition in the Strong's Hebrew. OT: 5048

Neged (neh'-ghed); from OT: 5046; a front, i.e. part opposite; specifically a **counterpart**, or mate; usually (adverbial, especially with preposition) over against or before:

KJV - about, (over) against, X aloof, X far (off), X from, over, presence, X **other side**, **sight**, X to **view.**
(Biblesoft's New Exhaustive Strong's Numbers and Concordance with Expanded Greek-Hebrew Dictionary. Copyright (c) 1994, Biblesoft and International Bible Translators, Inc.)

The female is the counterpart of male, not the counterfeit of male. The female is not an afterthought. She was created from the beginning just like the male was created. They were both in one body and in Genesis 5:1 we find that God called them both Adam. Now let me repeat this. Both male and female had one name because they were 'one flesh.'

The female sees things, once separated from the male, that

he cannot see. She is his other sight, his other side, his other view, not a second creation, but a separation of creation. There is much power in the ability to walk in agreement with someone who always has the 'other viewpoint!' And yet, herein lies the power that God has intended for humanity.

When we realize that we are made in the triune Godhead's image, then it is easier to see the value, the power that can be attained by two becoming one. What about triune? Triune would be three beings, not just two beings? Where is the third part, the tri part of the earth image of the Godhead?

I want you to see it the way that the Lord revealed it to me.

Triune Godhead

Father   Son   Holy Ghost

Duo mankind

Male   ?   Female

Again, my question remains the same. Where is the third part of our human image of a triune Godhead? We are supposed to be reflecting His image on the earth. How can we do that when we are a duet and the Godhead is a trio?

It is very easy to see that the male correlates or runs parallel with the Father aspect of the Godhead. It is also, relatively easy to see the correlation between the Holy Spirit as the female expression of God and the correlation of the female human.

Look at the scripture in Acts 2 where the Holy Spirit is given to the earth. He is the promise that comes after Jesus, just as the female is what comes after the male, in formation, not creation.

"When the day of Pentecost came, they were all together in one place. Suddenly a sound like the blowing of a violent wind came from heaven and filled the whole house where they were sitting. They saw what seemed to be tongues of fire that separated and came to rest on each of them. All of them were filled with the Holy Spirit and began to speak in other tongues as the Spirit enabled them." Acts 2:1-4 NIV.

"If you love Me, you will obey what I command. And I will ask the Father, and He will give you another Advocate to help you and be with you forever- the Spirit of truth. The world cannot accept Him, because it neither sees Him nor knows Him. But you know Him, for He lives with you and will be in you." John 14:15-18 NIV.

This is the promise from Jesus that the Holy Spirit, the Advocate and Counselor, our other sight, our other view, our other side, is given to us and that the Holy Spirit lives with us and is in us. The Holy Spirit comes out of the fire that fell on the heads of the people on the day of Pentecost in Acts 2. Thus, the feminine side of the trinity is the Holy Spirit.

"This message is sent to you by the one who has the seven-fold Spirit of God." Revelation 3:1 TLB.

The Amplified Bible reads like this *"These are the words of Him who has the seven Spirits of God [the sevenfold Holy Spirit]."* Revelation 3:1.

Now common sense would tell us all that this must be the feminine side of God because I have never known a male to be multifaceted, especially, seven faceted! Only women can put on their makeup, drive the car, talk on the cell phone, keep the kids in their seats, and drive through for breakfast, and counsel a friend all at the same time! Women are definitely the Holy Spirit side of the Godhead!

Let's take another look at it.

Father	Son	Holy Spirit
Male	?	Female

Is it coming any clearer to you? I think that we have established the two sides but the third one, the middle one is still missing.

That is pretty simple when you think about it. Remember vertical, not horizontal. In the 'natural' realm of the earth, horizontal is all our minds will do, but when we teach ourselves to think 'outside of the box' we can begin to get a clearer picture of things. When we realize that God tells us that we don't naturally think like He thinks. He tells us that our thoughts are lower than His thoughts, that our ways are not His ways. But that does not mean that He does not want us to think like He thinks. It just means that to think as He thinks we must think higher, on a different dimension, on a higher plane.

"For My thoughts are not your thoughts, nor are your ways My ways," says the LORD. "For as the heavens are higher than the earth, so are My ways higher than your ways, and My thoughts than your thoughts." Isaiah 55:8-9 NKJV.

"Again, truly I tell you that if two of you on earth agree about anything they ask for, it will be done for them by my Father in heaven. For where two or three come together in my name, there am I with them." Matthew 18:19-20 NIV.

Agreement is a legal summons from the earth to heaven. Agreement literally brings God on the scene in every situation. Agreement summons the One of the Godhead that was sent for us to come to us legally! Agreement completes the triune Godhead on the earth!

Now do you see it?

Father   Son   Holy Spirit
Male   Son   Female

So it really is vertical AND horizontal. When you draw a vertical and a horizontal line with an intersection you have made the 'sign' of the tav, the sign of the cross! Where our vertical and our horizontal thinking connect is the center of the cross. This is where the head of Jesus rested while He was being crucified.

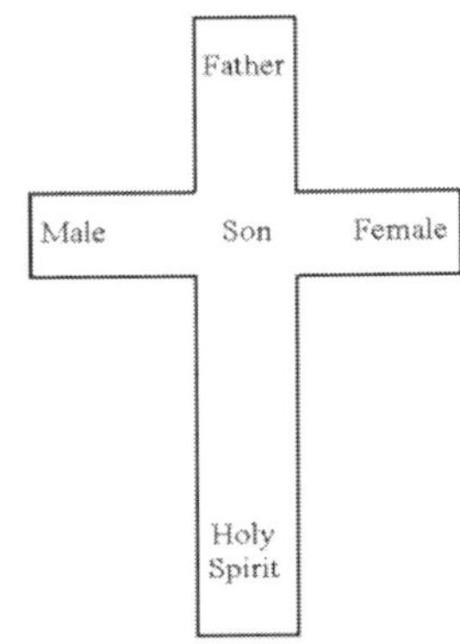

Jesus is our divine connection from the earth to heaven. Jesus is our sign, our road sign, and our road map to eternity. Jesus is our way, truth, and life.

When we decide to do this in our lives, our prayer life should change also. We should begin to understand the depth of the prayer that Jesus taught His disciples.

*"Our Father in heaven, hallowed be Your name. Your kingdom come, **Your will be done on earth as it is in heaven**. Give us this day our daily bread. And forgive us our debts, as we forgive our debtors. And do not lead us into temptation, but deliver us from the evil one. For Yours is the kingdom and the power and the glory forever. Amen."* Matthew 6:9-13.

Notice the highlighted part of this prayer. Jesus is trying to get us to realize that God's will is in heaven and that our job in prayer is to pray God's will to the earth.

"For My thoughts are not your thoughts, nor are your ways My ways," says the LORD. "For as the heavens are higher than the earth, so are My ways higher than your ways, and My thoughts than your thoughts " Isaiah 55:8-9.

Remember in the Hebrew language the male definition is, "His hand is in the midst of the fire." In the Hebrew female means, "What comes out of the fire." Each word, both male and female have three symbols when writing the actual words. Two of the symbols spell fire in both male and female. But there is a definite different symbol; the third symbol in the female script and the second symbol in the male script are totally different. Most people would immediately say that this is why we can't get along. This is why we can't understand each other; this is why we are so different!

But let's examine the two different symbols.

FIRE

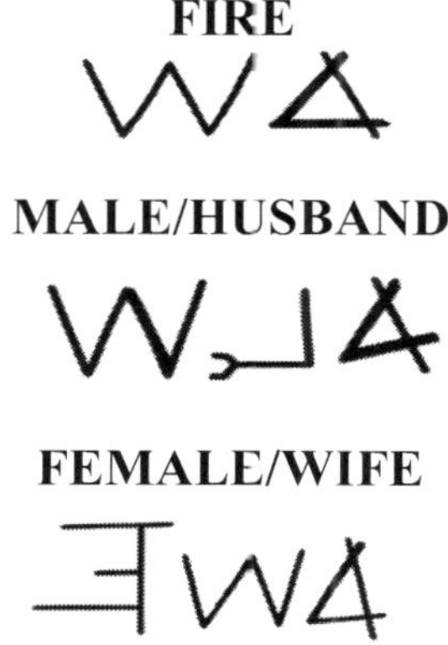

MALE/HUSBAND

FEMALE/WIFE

Take the two different symbols and let's isolate them. Let's put them together like they are in agreement.

GOD

These two symbols now spell a word. Quite simply put these two symbols spell GOD!

The exact word is Yah, defined as "The Lord in the land of the living."

By choosing to walk in agreement in our relationships between male and female it summons Jesus, the Lord in the land of the living, on the scene of our lives, our relationships, our marriages, and our homes!

When we can finally get it straight that the power of agreement in our marriage relationships can bring Jesus on the scene, our divine connector, then and only then, are we truly the image of God, triune, three in one. Now we can reflect the light and image of our Triune God on the earth for all humanity to see.

Male   Son   Female

This is the fulfillment of Genesis 1:26-27.

Chapter Four
The Circle of Threes

A three-fold cord is not easily broken. We see this truth written in the Book of Ecclesiastes and it is understood when we tie a braid of three cords together to make a string, or a rope stronger. Our lives are no different. There are three threads or strings that can be tied together with time that can finish and complete our earthly lives, making it stronger.

Notice similar patterns of threes, circles that complete and finish a timeline. There is a definite change for the earth during Noah's time.

Before Flood	During Flood	After Flood
Sin	Purification	New Beginnings
Before Blood	During Blood	After Blood
Innocence	Realization Of Sin	Overcome Sin

Before Seed   During Seed   After Seed

Before Germination During Germination After Germination

Before Trial   During Trial   After Trial

I could go on and on, because the earth was created and according to the scripture on the third day of creation this principle was implemented.

Seed   Time   Harvest

This is a three-fold circle in life that defines everything from the beginning to the end of all things. Some seeds are planted and very quickly we see the harvest. But nonetheless, 'time' will always be the second stage, no matter how quickly or slowly we see the harvest. Time may be little, or time may be much. But time is an integral part of all fulfillment of the third stage of life's harvest.

A woman's natural life (and a man's too, just not as visible) has three distinct stages.

Before blood (before menstruation)
During blood (menstruation)
After blood (menopause)

Jesus' life can be seen in the same way.

Before the cross (birth-Garden of Gethsemane)
During the cross (Three days He bled)
After the cross (victory, no more blood, eternity)

Later we will discuss these three distinct phases of life.
Passive   Active   Authoritative

These three line up with the ones we will discuss in this next chapter. I just want you to be introduced to these three-step stages of life so that later on you can recall how it flows with these other patterns.

We tend to think in terms of the stages of our lives as the last one, the after blood stage, being the unproductive stage. And yet, when you look at the entire scheme of things, the most productive time is always going to be the final stage, the 'after blood,' the menopause for women, the after midlife for men.

Of course, we can parallel a man's life in much the same way.

Before voice change (before puberty)

During voice change (during puberty)

After voice change (after puberty)

(This is an unusual time for both the male and the female. Hormones are raging, identifying feelings, emotions, etc. This is the time when we must learn to crucify the flesh or be ruled by it for the rest of our lives! Then after we crucify our screaming flesh for gratification, our hormones begin to settle down, we can think rationally again, and make decisions based upon our hearts and not our flesh instincts.)

This is where the scripture comes in that tells us what to do.

"Train a child in the way he should go, and when he is old he will not turn from it. The rich rule over the poor, and the borrower is servant to the lender." Proverbs 22:6-7 NIV.

Training a child will help him or her make the correct choices when faced with their own desires that are against what they know in their hearts.

It would be so nice if the Bible had given an exact age. Instead, the wording says, 'and when he is old.' This is because progression in life is our choice. It is not by design but by choice. I grow up when I choose. Others grow up when they choose. Old is a relative term. I have known people at twelve to be very 'old,' very grown up. Others don't seem to grow up until they are in their 30's; others in their 40's, and some don't seem to ever grow up!

Most children can hardly wait to grow up and then when one becomes an adult they spend their lives longing to be children again.

We must learn to embrace the present rather than looking back or ahead. Training takes time. It is not telling a child once, but a continual training, telling, correcting and retelling. Training can only be done with the element of time involved. Without time there really is no training.

When our son, Harry III, was just a young boy, he wanted to play t-ball like the other children. My husband, Harry, was a great athlete, especially in baseball. Of course, we encouraged our son to play and be a part of a team. One day we were watching him play, and he was not very good.

He didn't pay attention. He was playing in the outfield and the color of the sky, the birds flying over head, the movement and shape of the clouds, even the clover in the grass were much more important to him than the slow pace of this ball game.

My husband was appalled. How could this be his son? His love for the sport should be enough for both of them, and certainly our son should have gotten some of his dad's genes to play baseball well!

When we arrived home, Harry (father) took Harry (son) outside in the backyard to practice this wonderful sport. Harry III was so thrilled to be playing with his dad, but, of course, he didn't know *how* to play yet. After several moments of trying to throw and catch the ball, father Harry came into the house and said to me, "How can he not know how to throw a ball? How can he not know how to hit the ball? I just don't understand it."

It dawned on me that no one had ever worked with him or taught him. Of course, he had seen it several times, seen others do it, even seen his dad do it, but no one had taken the time to train him to do it!

Training is time consuming. I learned this when it came time to 'potty train' our children. I learned very quickly that the real person who is being trained is the parent. The parent must learn to be totally and completely focused on the clock, noticing the minutes as they go by. On the first day, every fifteen minutes our child had to be set down on the potty chair, read to, talked to, and interacted with for a few minutes. Then fifteen minutes later we had to try again, without criticism, judgment, or scolding.

Every so often our child would have a little 'tinkle,' probably quite by accident! When this would happen we had a big parade, a big 'mama' band would play, and the festivities began! Then in fifteen minutes we did it all again! This was exhausting the first day!

The second day we did exactly the same thing except we spaced the time out to thirty minutes. The third day we went to every hour. By the end of three days all three of our children were trained. Well, I should say, two of our children were trained. I didn't learn this until after I failed miserably with our first son, Harry! He finally got it, but it was not with any help from me! I forced the start time and he was too young, only a year old. Timing is everything. If we lag behind everyone suffers; if we rush ahead everyone suffers. God's timing is perfect in all things.

After Roman was born and it was time to train him, I decided to get some advice from a woman who had run a successful daycare for many years. I talked to her and asked her how many children had she potty trained. The number was astounding to me, in the hundreds!

I was shocked! She still had all of her hair, she still looked sane, and she was still walking and talking normally! How did she do it?   I asked her, with a sarcastic air of 'surely all children are not easy,' and the attitude of, 'you haven't met our son, Harry.' She answered me with a laugh in her voice and a big smile on her face as if to say she had heard mother after mother say those same exact words!

She said, "It is not the child who has to be potty trained. It is the parent. The parent must learn to completely focus on the child for three days, no distractions. There can be no leaving the house, no errands, no lunches, no shopping, no phone, or watching television, no computer, nothing! Focus must be maintained at all times BY THE PARENT!" She went on to say, "When the parent is ready to potty train the child will easily join in."

Of course, there were three signs that a parent needed to recognize in a child before the process should ever begin. Once a child had shown these three signs, then training could be entered into successfully.

For the male reader right now, you could care less what the three signs are, but for the mother, grandmother, and aunt reader, they are holding their breath now, waiting for me to tell what these three signs are!

First, a child needs to be able to communicate verbally that they need to go to the bathroom.

Second, a child needs to be able to wake up from a nap regularly with a dry diaper, indicating that they are learning to control the 'let down' mechanism of the bladder.

Third, a child needs to be able to recognize the social need for correct potty habits; for example, they are embarrassed to go to the bathroom out in the open, hide behind a chair when they go in their diaper, etc.

Regardless, of the procedure, time is the key. Nothing is gained on this earth without time.

"As long as the earth endures, seed time and harvest, cold and heat, winter and summer, day and night will never cease." Genesis 8:22 NIV.

I have noticed that when things happen in our lives, when we are tried by circumstances, situations, trials, trouble, and problems, we tend to grow up much faster. We could call these times the 'fire of God' times. When faced with the 'fire' do we run into it asking God to change us, or do we run screaming in the night to 'get me out of here?' Whichever we choose tends to predict the next place of our lives, the next level, or the repeat of the same 'trip around the tree.'

Without a doubt life comes in stages. A house is not built in a day, nor is a life built without a life 'time.' There is that word again, 'time.' We can never seem to get away from it. Time is a vital part of the plan for our lives here on this earth.

Chapter Five
The Passive Stage

Passive is almost a dirty word in our society. Especially, my generation is all about being productive, goal setting, and achieving!   And yet, as I have spent quiet time in the presence of God I have never once had Him say to me how proud He is of my earthly accomplishments.   Rather, just being still in His presence makes me feel His greater approval.

My desire to be near Him, to be still and listen, whether He is saying anything or not, seems to be more what He wants for my life.   There is much to be said about passivity that is not negative when it applies to the necessary stage of life where we develop trust, our true identity in Christ, instead of our identity based upon our own accomplishments. I truly believe that God does not judge us on what we accomplish but rather what we overcome.

Let's look at the stage called 'passive' in the light of the natural set of circumstances surrounding it.   As a little child

God says that we may approach Him. So, there must be a very valuable lesson that we must first learn in this first stage of life.

In a female's life it is so easily seen. 'Before blood' is an appropriate natural term to define this passive, inactive first stage. Then there is the stage defined as 'during blood' and of course, let's not forget the third and final stage, 'after blood.'

These can readily be seen in a woman's life because of menstruation. As we mentioned earlier, they are, also, in a man's life which we also mentioned.

Before Puberty (voice high and innocent)

During Puberty (voice begins to change and hormones begin to rage)

After Puberty (voice settles down, hormones settle down, age of maturity begins)

This is the easiest place to see these three stages, in the evolution of the physical body. But these three phases are also in every area of our lives. We transition between these three stages in our souls, (minds, wills, emotions,) and in our spirits. We grow up, mature, evolve, like a butterfly through the metamorphosis process into the mature adults that we are purposed and created to be.

I have called this stage of 'before blood,' as the passive stage. This seems to be fairly accurate when you think of it. We are not (re)productive in our physical bodies. We cannot reproduce life in this stage. We quite readily trust people. We enjoy life at it's fullest. Hardly ever do you find a child who is carrying the weight of the world on his or her shoulders in this early stage of life. It is an easy time, a trusting time, a 'not a care in this world' time for most children.

It is in this level, or stage, or phase that our belief system is put into place.   What we believe begins during this time in our lives.   Later on what we believe is tested and tried, through the trials of life, but certainly most belief systems start in our minds and hearts during this stage of life.

Harry told in his book, 'The Orphan Generation; Longing For A Father,' of the story of his dad setting him at the back door of their car dealership when he was just a little boy.   Each weekend he would get to go to work with his dad on Saturday. Each weekend his dad would put him in a different department to learn the inner workings of the business.   This particular Saturday his dad sat him at the back door to watch and learn.   At the end of the day Harry learned that people took things out the back door that didn't belong to them! He noticed those people stole from his dad's business.

I have heard my husband say a million times in our decades of marriage.   "It's not what comes in the front door that matters, but what goes out the backdoor that can break you financially."   Harry learned to be a good businessman in the passive stage of his life by observing the actions of others. Harry is an anointed businessman because he allowed the Lord to begin to teach and train him in the very first stage of his life. We all can learn lessons as a child if we pay attention and accept the consequences of our choices and actions.

When I was a little girl we lived way out in the country and I had one little girlfriend.   Her name was Georgia Mae Burdine.   She was our next-door neighbor, which was several miles away.   Her family and my family would 'visit' once or twice a week.   She and I loved these times because we would go off and play by ourselves! We both had huge imaginations and we could come up with some amazing adventures!

We always stayed close enough to the porch so we could hear when the parents would start 'wrapping up the visit' and begin to talk about going home. Once that announcement was made, she and I would run as fast as we could and hide so we could prolong the visit! Of course, we got a lot of spankings because of this behavior but it never seemed to be enough punishment to stop the behavior.

One time we hid behind the septic tank (yep, that's where we hid) and there was a bunch of poison ivy there. We didn't know those leaves were poison ivy so with our massive imaginations we used the leaves for powder puffs! We powdered just about every inch of our bodies from our heads to our toes! Did we learn our lesson yet? Nope!

Another time, we hid in the freshly cut pine tree logs, seeping their sap! It was so sticky and got everywhere; all in our hair and on our skin! My mama washed my hair in kerosene trying to get the sticky substance out of my hair. I never realized until then how much hair was on my arms and legs! We both looked like we were tarred and feathered! What a mess!

I don't remember when we stopped hiding, but it wasn't for a very long time. No matter how much trouble we got ourselves into we just kept doing the same wonderful things over and over. We were in the passive (unproductive, very much enjoying) stage of life.

There is a story from the Bible that I would assume many people know. But as I studied this all too familiar story, I began to notice a pattern in a certain little girl's life that I had never seen before.

There was a little orphaned girl named Mary. She was from

a nowhere town with a 'been nowhere' past, and a 'going nowhere' future. Her mother, Anne, had tried very hard to rear her in the ways of the Lord.   Even as a single parent Anne had given Mary the greatest gift of all in life. She had shown her the Messiah, the One who would deliver the nation of Israel from the doom and destruction in which it was headed.

Anne had talked of the Messiah, the deliverer, all of Mary's life; so much so that Mary had given her heart, her future, to this unseen, foretold, mystery King of the Jews. He was not a flesh Deliverer, no, never!   He was the promised One, written about down through the ages, chronicled throughout the Book, the Torah.

Each day as her chores were finished, she would look for a quiet spot so that she could pour out her heart to this unseen Savior of her people. She would wander out in the fields so she could be alone with her thoughts and find 'Peace.' As the solitude would envelope her she would always begin to pour out her dreams, desires, plans, and hopes for her future to her unseen Peacekeeper.

The more she spent time with this invisible Man-God her mother had filled her head and heart with, the more she could feel Him all around her. She would talk to Him, sharing her vision, her desires and hopes, her ultimate dreams.   She would listen so intently to her heart and her soul where she had learned He would talk back to her. She was learning to worship Him from the depths of her being.

Mary was developing into a young teenage girl.   She was beginning to change in her body and with these changes came a change in her prayers and her focus.   From the first time she had shared her most intimate thoughts with her God, her Lord, she had not been afraid. She felt comforted, secure, and safe. She felt as if this God had become a father to her, one who would listen and counsel with her best interest at heart.

One day she was out in the field just lying back on the grass looking at the sky giving her heart more and more to the God of this marvelous universe, when she felt compelled to open her eyes. Someone was here with her. Someone had invaded her quiet time with her God!

She slowly raised her head and opened her eyes. As she did, she was almost blinded by the magnificence of this most powerful being standing before her! She quickly jumped to her feet, stumbling backward as this creature's mere size was overpowering to her! And yet, she was not really afraid. There was a peace, calmness, about this warrior like figure that was disarming.

As she gathered her thoughts and righted her tumbling body, the creature that was illuminating a great and powerful light began to speak to Mary. What he said was so incredible and life changing, not just for Mary, but also for all mankind. So much so was this powerful moment in history that it has been written for all to see in every translation of the Bible.

"Now in the sixth month the angel Gabriel was sent by God to a city of Galilee named Nazareth, to a virgin betrothed to a man whose name was Joseph, of the house of David. The virgin's name was Mary. And having come in, the angel said to her, 'Rejoice, highly favored one, the Lord is with you; blessed are you among women!' But when she saw him, she was troubled at his saying, and considered what manner of greeting this was. Then the angel said to her, 'Do not be afraid, Mary, for you have found favor with God. And behold, you will conceive in your womb and bring forth a Son, and shall call His name JESUS. He will be great, and will be called the Son of the Highest; and the Lord God will give Him the throne of His father David. And He will

reign over the house of Jacob forever, and of His kingdom there will be no end.'

Then Mary said to the angel, 'How can this be, since I do not know a man?' And the angel answered and said to her, 'The Holy Spirit will come upon you, and the power of the Highest will overshadow you; therefore, also, that Holy One who is to be born will be called the Son of God.

Now indeed, Elizabeth your relative has also conceived a son in her old age; and this is now the sixth month for her who was called barren. For with God nothing will be impossible.' Then Mary said, 'Behold the maidservant of the Lord! Let it be to me according to your word.' And the angel departed from her." Luke 1:26-38.

In just twelve verses an entire universal scene changed through the acceptance and submission of one little girl just barely in her second 'active stage' of life. Her acceptance of God's plan for her life over her own ideas and thoughts on the matter of her future was so evident in this story that we can see the ultimate plan for all of mankind.

Mary had her own ideas and plans in motion. She was in our society a very young girl, just beginning the second stage of life. She was just old enough to begin her monthly period. In our day and age, she was much too young to even consider being engaged and married, but in the time in which she lived, by the time one was bleeding, the time had come for her to be married.

Once the blood came each month then the society had determined that pregnancy was possible. so a female's ultimate job was to produce the babies for the family and fulfill her destiny. Mary had just begun this second stage of life , so she was engaged to Joseph to be married in the very near future.

Her first stage of life was so simple and wonderful. She was not bleeding; she could not reproduce babies in her body. She was just to be and let be. She could do what was expected of her in the family and then her time was her own. She could dream and think out loud. She could lie on her back and stare at the sky night or day and no one would think anything of it. She was a little girl and that is what little girls do! She was totally and completely passive, no reproduction involved in her life.

She was not expected to reproduce another generation yet. She was not expected to work hard and take care of a husband, a home, and a family yet. She did not have to deal with the monthly discomfort of a menstrual cycle yet. Her body was not producing a life receiving egg yet. She was just being and dreaming of the future in this passive stage. No one expected anything more.

Chapter Six
The Active Stage

We left our story in the last chapter with Mary as a little passive girl out in the field. Nothing was really expected of her yet by those around her who loved her.   But her heart had already been turned to God. No one really knew the intimate conversations that had already transpired between little passive Mary and her Almighty, All Powerful God. She had already fallen in love with her soon coming King and He hadn't been sent to the earth yet!

This day looked like every other day except that Mary's hormones were changing, and that meant her heart was being pulled toward the completion of a husband in her life. She had many long and meaningful conversations with her God about this very duty in her near future. Her spiritual heart had already been given to this unseen God of Israel, and her natural desires were being turned toward Joseph, whom she was now betrothed.

As she lay on the grass staring into the clouds trying to see into the future for her life, this huge angel named Gabriel interrupted her.   I am sure at first, she was not sure who or even what this great and magnificent creature standing before her was. The light coming out of this being was almost blinding and she had to let her eyes adjust to the brilliance of his presence before she could even look directly at him.

Fear began to rise up in her as her mind raced. She must have begun to think such thoughts as, "I am just a lowly little girl from the region of Galilee, from a little town called Nazareth. What have I done to bring such an awesome creature into my little world out here in the field?"

But immediately, this angel who was sent from God to bring her heaven's message, began to speak to her and answer every question she was contemplating. He was reading her thoughts! Just the very presence of this being was overwhelming and yet somehow, comforting at the same time.

He spoke in a language she understood, and yet, at the same time, his words were dimensional, like they were coming in waves. These waves were of thoughts that were beyond her ability to comprehend at that moment. Mary thought to herself, "I hear what he is saying, but please, slow down. My mind cannot receive this all at once!"

The angel sent from God first began to tell her whom she was. This was not based on what she knew about herself, or her environment. This was not based on what family she had been born into or the color of her skin. This knowledge of who Mary was from the throne room of God was not based on the economic status of her home and family or even how well she was doing in school.

When this angel began to tell her who she really was this knowledge came from the very heart of God who knows us all better than we know ourselves. This knowledge was not based upon Mary's past or anything she had ever done right or wrong, but was formulated from the heart of the worshiper Mary had become as she listened to her mother and chose her future by receiving her Messiah in her heart.

We each make our own futures based upon our present choices, as we simply decide who is our Redeemer, who owns us, whose name do we bear. I have chosen my Messiah, and He is my Redeemer King Jesus. I am His and He is mine. Just like Mary I worked this out very early in my passive stage of life. It's not too late for you.

The angel told Mary that she was favored above all other women. This revelation was not about anything to do with her background or her past, but this favored position that the angel was speaking of had to do with the very near future for Mary. God had already been with Mary in her future. He already knew before He sent Gabriel that Mary would choose to obey the command of God and that she would totally and completely submit to the will of the Father for her life.

That is why God said through the angel Gabriel that Mary was favored above all other women! In God, in the future, Mary had already accepted God's plan and was already pregnant with the Messiah, God's Son! It was already finished in Mary's future.

The word 'favored' has a definite and direct meaning that we need not miss in this text. Without much thought we can see that it means that Mary was set apart and chosen for a great mission from God. We know this because we know the rest of the story. There will never be another woman in the entire universe throughout history like Mary for she is the only woman ever chosen to birth the Messiah to the world.

But let's look a little deeper and see what else is hidden in this text for us! Revelation is always hidden within the pages of God's Word, not hidden from us, but hidden for us!   It always takes a little deeper digging to find those precious nugget revelations the Lord has hidden for us to find!

Strong's NT: 5487 Charitoo (khar-ee-to'-o), from NT: 5485, to grace, i.e. indue with special honor:

KJV - make accepted, be highly favored.

The definition and word above come from this word.

Strong's NT: 5485 Charis (khar'-ece); from NT: 5463; graciousness (as gratifying), of manner or act (abstract or concrete; literal, figurative or spiritual; especially the divine influence upon the heart, and its reflection in the life; including gratitude):

KJV - acceptable, benefit, favor, gift, grace (-ious), joy, liberality, pleasure, thank (-s, -worthy).

TO BE GRACIOUS, SHOW FAVOR

Strong's OT: 2580 Chen, "favor; grace."

The basic meaning of Chen is "favor." Whatever is "pleasant and agreeable" can be described by this word.

Chen also denotes the response to whatever is "*agreeable*." The verbs used with "favor" are: "*give favor*" Genesis 39:21, "*obtain favor*" Exodus 3:21, and "*find favor*" Genesis 6:8, RSV. The idioms are equivalent to the English verbs "to like" or "to love": "[She] said to him, *"Why have I found favor in your eyes, that you should take notice of me, when I am a foreigner?"* Ruth 2:10, RSV. (From Vine's Expository Dictionary of Biblical Words, Copyright (c) 1985, Thomas Nelson Publishers.)

As you can see when the angel Gabriel spoke to Mary and used the word 'favor' concerning the way God felt about her, he was setting her apart from all other women, a divine placement and position that was being offered to her.

The beauty of God is that He already knows what we will choose in the future so in His offering anything or doing anything to us or for us He already knows our response! He knew that when the angel Gabriel brought the divine revelation of the plan of God for Mary's future to her, she would submit her own ideas, thoughts, and dreams just to obey God.   She submitted her plan, and we know that she had plans, because she was engaged to Joseph.   We also, know she had plans because she was a girl and girls always have many plans and dreams!

Once God gave her His plan, His desire for her future, she obediently and willingly laid down her concepts, plans, ideas, dreams, and visions, and accepted His future plan and knowledge for her life.

By her obedience and submission to God's will for her life she spiritually transitioned from the passive stage of life into the active stage of her life. This was the stage where covenant was taken, blood was shed, whether symbolically or literally, or both. Since Mary was already engaged to Joseph, she had probably already begun her monthly periods.

She accepted God's plan for her future and the overshadowing of the Holy Spirit impregnated her and she became able to produce a virgin birth fruit from her favored womb. She accepted the Seed of life into her fertile womb and in just a little time, forty weeks later, (the end of testing and trial) she delivered a Son, not just any son, but the Son of the Most High God!

Once she became the mother of Jesus in the natural sense of the word she began to bleed again with her monthly periods. This active stage has no exact time frame just as the passive stage is not specific across the board of humanity. Each stage of life is unique to each individual.

When our son, Harry III, was starting to school I was the type of mother who wanted to know specifics.   When will he read? When will he write? When will his motor skills be developed?   And on and on the questions went.   I must have been that type of parent that a teacher hated to see coming for they knew the moment I got close enough for them to hear me the questions would begin.

In the early years of Harry's schooling he had the most wonderful teacher.   Her name was Deloris Mayfield.   She taught a grade between kindergarten and first grade called developmental first grade. We thought this would be a wonderful experience for Harry III and it turned out to be just that!   Mostly because of Mrs. Mayfield, I think, for she was the most patient, the kindest, the most accepting, and wisest woman I have ever met.

Each day as I would pick Harry III up from school, I would be full of questions for her.   My nature was to observe other children and then the comparisons would begin.   "Mrs. Mayfield, when will Harry write like so and so?   When will Harry be able to tie his shoes?   When will Harry read?" Each question was answered the same way day after day. Mrs. Mayfield with all her deserved wisdom would say, "When he is ready."

That was not a very satisfying answer to me!   I wanted a time frame. I wanted exacts! Life is not about exacts. Life is designed specifically for each individual.   We determine the time frame of the journey of the pattern of our lives by how much we are led by the Spirit of God, or how much we are led by earthly life comparisons, questions, carnal thinking and being and sometimes, time is just a part of the process no matter what we do or don't do.

The passive stage of life has a definite beginning, when we are born. But the transition into the active stage is based upon our process, our acceptance of the future, and a deep desire to follow after God no matter what the cost. It is a process. It is a journey.

We can't embrace the promise and ignore the process.

For everything there is a season, and time is our friend throughout each season of life. Mary began to bleed again during the birthing of God's Son, Jesus. This began the bleeding process that would continue until she became productive again.

If you parallel that statement to our lives you can see that spiritually when we are not productive, many times we feel like all we are doing is bleeding. Sometimes we feel like we are bleeding out! We feel weak, dehydrated, and no energy. But God has a plan for our future no matter what stage we find ourselves. Instead of us bleeding out, we are designed to bleed through. The blood of Jesus bleeds through us until that is all that is visible.

Even though Mary had followed the plan of God for her life, her reputation was ruined. It did not matter that Joseph married her even though she was pregnant by the Holy Spirit overshadowing her; people talked about her for the rest of her natural life. She laid down what others thought of her to obey the plan of God. Her life became about God-pleasing, and not people-pleasing.

Was there really no room at the inn or was her reputation preceding her to the point that they would not give them a room? She gave birth to the Most High God in a stable so that prophecy could be fulfilled.

Thirty years passed, but she held on to the promise of God through the bleeding stage of her life. Mary was thirty years older, probably around forty-three or forty-four. This is just an estimate but it's close because she was just starting her teenage years, just beginning to be reproductive and have her monthly periods when the angel Gabriel spoke to her. Thirty years later we can see the rest of the story for it is history.

Chapter Seven
The Authoritative Stage

"On the third day there was a wedding in Cana of Galilee, and the mother of Jesus was there. Now both Jesus and His disciples were invited to the wedding. And when they ran out of wine, the mother of Jesus said to Him, 'They have no wine.' Jesus said to her, 'Woman, what does your concern have to do with Me? My hour has not yet come.' His mother said to the servants, 'Whatever He says to you, do it.' Now there were set there six water pots of stone, according to the manner of purification of the Jews, containing twenty or thirty gallons apiece. Jesus said to them, 'Fill the water pots with water.' And they filled them up to the brim. And He said to them, 'Draw some out now, and take it to the master of the feast.' And they took it.

When the master of the feast had tasted the water that was made wine and did not know where it came from (but the servants who had drawn the water knew), the master of the feast called the bridegroom. And he said to him, 'Every man at the beginning sets out the good wine, and when the guests have well drunk, then the inferior. You have kept the good wine until now!' This beginning of signs Jesus did in Cana of Galilee, and manifested His glory; and His disciples believed in Him." John 2:1-11.

In the above story notice the time frame that was given. The story begins for Mary on the third day. She is about to make a divine transition from being the mother to being the bride. She is about to transition from the active stage to the third and final stage of her life's journey.

This is a prophetic time frame in God's timetable. If you have studied with me for any length of time, you know that I love the ancient Hebrew language and you also know that I love numbers and their meanings. The number 3 is defined as bride in the ancient numerical language simply because in the Jewish tradition all weddings happened on the third day of the week!

Most people equate the third day with the word resurrection and that would be a positive and correct assumption. The third day has a defining moment in history for all the modern-day church. The third day is resurrection for our lives, not just the life of Jesus. But because Jesus, the Son of God arose from the grave on the third day, then we can also embrace a type of rebirth, resurrection, and experience in our own individual lives. In the next chapter we will discuss the application and revelation of what this third day really represents for all of us.

When we combine the thoughts of the third day representing the bride and resurrection then we can tie them together, and consider that it is the dying of the bride's past on the wedding day to become a resurrected bride with a new name, a new destiny, a new bloodline, and a new future!

Then notice not only was a time frame given but also an event was taking place. This was a time for a wedding! In the modern-day Christian church we are supposed to be looking for our Bridegroom to come and take us to the wedding feast.

The first mention of any guests to this wedding was the mother of Jesus. She was not referred to as Mary in this passage of scripture, but the mother of Jesus. This reference was not an oversight of her name but rather to give us what stage of life that she was in. Mary was the 'mother of Jesus' therefore she was still in the active stage of her life as she first came to this wedding.

Jesus and his disciples were also invited. I have found this to be quite interesting. Throughout the New Testament Jesus is the main character of the Bible, the star of the play, so to speak. But in this passage of scripture Mary was mentioned before Jesus. Why would this be?

This story was about Mary. This chapter is such a wonderful historical chapter for us in that it was the first of many miracles that Jesus performed in his three-year ministry. It was the beginning of his earthly ministry.

When I first began to study the life of Jesus in relationship to the three stages of life I thought when Jesus entered His ministry that He entered the active stage of his life, but upon further thought and prayer, I realized He hadn't started to bleed yet.

This is a prophetic chapter, not just about history but about the future also. This is a future glance at the bride of Christ and our Bridegroom, the final culmination of a lifetime search for our fulfilled completion.

Now let me ask you a question. For there to be a successful

wedding one must have two willing participants, correct? There must be a bridegroom and a bride. But in all actuality who is the focus primarily on at any wedding? Is it the bridegroom or the bride?

Of course, it is the bride! The bridegroom is necessary, but all eyes are on the bride! She is adorned in beauty, covered in gorgeous fabrics and jewels. God loves to adorn His bride. We find a reference to God adorning the bride in the prophetic Book of Ezekiel in chapter sixteen. Right down to the crown that God places on the head of the bride, we see what we would term a veil, or headpiece!

Let's think about this a minute. Stop and meditate on this. Do you see why the mother of Jesus was mentioned before Jesus and His disciples? Because this was the third day, the wedding day, the day of the bride! Even the thought that Jesus did His very first miracle on the day of the bride should show us a beautiful picture of who we are to Christ! Even His first act as Messiah was done on 'our day, the day of the bride!'

The word 'third' in the Strong's OT: 5154 Nechuwshah (nekh-oo-shaw'); or nechushah (nekh-oo-shaw'); feminine of OT: 5153; copper:

KJV - brass, steel. Compare OT: 5176.
(Biblesoft's New Exhaustive Strong's Numbers and Concordance with Expanded Greek-Hebrew Dictionary. Copyright © 1994, 2003 Biblesoft, Inc. and International Bible Translators, Inc.)

Third means feminine. The third day is about the 'feminine.' What could that possibly mean? It means that the third day in the time frame of history is about the preparation and purification of the bride of Christ. The third day is the wedding day, and the resurrection day. It is about the bride!

When Jesus arose on the third day and the Bible made reference that Jesus endured the cross for the promise that was set before Him, we must think in terms of a bride and Bridegroom. What promise could have been set before Jesus that He would endure the torture, the pain, and the excruciating punishment that He endured?

What could have been in His future vision that was so compelling, so powerful, that He would push through that crucifixion process and never give up, never call forth 10,000 angels to come and deliver Him? What or who could have been so joyously set before His vision that He would allow Himself to be tortured to death?

What was before Him in His future that He did not have in His past? What was He seeing? When a bridegroom stands at the altar and watches the bride coming down the isle, he only has eyes for her. Even if the walls fell down, and the ceiling caved in, the bridegroom only sees the promise that is set before him.

As Jesus endured the cross, the horrible crucifixion, the torture, the pain, He only had eyes for His bride! The bride was the promise set before Him. His passion then and even today is still the same. Jesus' passion is for His bride!

This passage of scripture can be seen on many levels, but if you look at it with prophetic future eyes you will see that this story is about today, right now in the time frame of history! This historical story about a bride is actually about you, His bride.

What are we doing to prepare ourselves for His coming? Are we ready? Are our wicks trimmed, and our vessels filled with oil? Are we without spot or wrinkle? Are we the promise that is set before Him? Are we His joy? Am I? Are you?

We, the bride, are His promise. Jesus, our Bridegroom, is our promise. Do we have enough passion for Him; are we totally and completely in love with Him to the point that our only vision is for Him? Is He all that you see as you progress down the 'aisle' of life?

Mary made a statement that gives us a sign that she was about to pass from the active stage of life into the third and final stage. She had accepted the call of God for her life. She had laid down her reputation in this earthly realm and walked the road that God had set before her. It was some thirty years later, and Mary had done the best she knew how to rear Jesus as her son, but most importantly, as the Messiah, the soon coming King, for the Jews.

The angel spoke to her in dimensions on that day almost thirty-one years earlier, and she had spent her life meditating, pondering, thinking and praying on the eternal thoughts that were placed in her spirit on that fateful day. God speaks to us in a vertical dimension that can only be processed through time, prayer, and much quiet meditation. As we progress, mature, and grow in God He then allows our eyes to see and our ears to hear what the Spirit of God is continually saying to us.

By this point, Mary knew something. This day, like every day of her natural life, was already shown to her, inside of her by the Holy Spirit. She knew what even Jesus didn't know yet. She knew it was time. She knew He had to begin His journey to the cross to fulfill His destiny. She was the ultimate mother in this story as she pushed her son, God's Son, to the cross.

When she arose that morning, her first thought was probably not about this wedding that they were going to attend, nor could she have imagined in her natural mind what was about to historically take place!   But as her thoughts turned toward her God and she began her daily routine of thinking and meditating on the things of God, eternal things, not what people think or say, but what is my Father, my God, saying today?

As she questioned, listened, and obeyed with her mind and heart, she began to see this day already fulfilled.   Her heart leaped with joy knowing that some things were going to be finished today. I can just hear her say out of her mouth she uttered three simple words, "It is finished."   God heard her prayer in the heavenlies, and He agreed. As Mary approached the wedding, her body was tingling all over, knowing something, yet not quite sure what she knew; but she knew something was about to happen!

I had a glimpse into this when I was seventeen years old. My family had a car wreck when I was eleven years old and it had left me with a short left leg.   I had limped for six years.   I had been hungry for God for many years and had just recently gotten a greater hunger to be whole, and to be all that God had called me to be. The milkman had brought a word from God when I was five or six years old that 'Someday, little girl, you are going to be Miss America,' and I had held on to those words, and I believed him!

To be Miss America I needed two legs the same length. It was a Monday morning, Oct. 21, 1974, and I was a senior at Weir High School. I was crippled by some standards in that one leg was shorter than the other for the past six years. I tried not to limp, and my mom hemmed all my pant legs shorter on the left side, but some days there was just no hiding the fact that the accident had left its mark on my future. But this day as I rose early and prepared for school, it was as if the Holy Spirit was whispering in my ear, "Today is your day. For this is the day you have waited."

I had made plans to drive with several people from town (we lived eight miles outside of town in the country on a dirt road) to a meeting in the big city of Jackson, MS.   It was several hours away so we would leave right after school so that we could get better seats in the auditorium.

A man by the name of Kenneth Hagin was speaking that evening on the topic of faith and my friends had told me that he also prayed for the sick.   I was not sick but my leg was shorter, and I really would like to believe that God wanted me to have two legs the same length to accomplish His plan of becoming Miss America for His glory.

That day, all day, my spirit was so excited.   I had spent the past six years trying to take any attention off the fact that my left leg was shorter than my right, but that day, I felt compelled to show everyone how much shorter my left leg was than my right leg.

I spent most of the day on the hall floor with my hips pressed up against the wall and my legs stretched out in front of me, feet extended.   Everyone could see that my left heel was almost two inches shorter than my right heel.

The evening service came, and we were all seated as close to the front as we could get. We were on the third row of the right side of the auditorium facing the platform.   I was the youngest, so I sat inside several seats toward the middle while the men sat on the end of the row.

Brother Hagin preached on faith. He always preached on faith. No matter what the subject was, or the title of the message was, or the scripture reference, it always came back to the topic of faith.   He was anointed to preach faith and when you were in his service you listened and learned about faith.

The end of the service approached, and Brother Hagin gave the invitation for salvation first.   Then he started the invitation for those who needed to be prayed for healing.   I had waited all day for this moment.   I knew that I knew that I knew that God was going to heal me this very night.

I had been studying my Bible for about six weeks deciding what I truly believed.   You see one must do this to truly walk with God. You must decide, figure out, what do you believe?   I am not talking about what religion you are involved with or what your pastor or your church believes. I am not talking about what your mama or your daddy believes.   I am talking about this simple thing; what do you believe?

I came home from school each day and got my Bible and my notebook. I opened to Matthew and started reading. When I came to a verse on healing, faith, or a miracle, I would write it out in my notebook. I wrote the reference and every word of the verse. Then I would keep reading and studying. I did this every day, day after day, for weeks. The Word of God will settle for you what nothing else can settle. It wasn't long before I knew that I knew that I knew that I believed in miracles. I believed in the power of Jesus. I believed in using my faith to receive what Jesus had already done for me. I had worked out my salvation and my belief system for this very moment in my life.   I was ready to receive my miracle.

When the altar call was given for healing, I jumped up out of my seat, made my way across the folks I had come to this service with, and I went straight to the middle of the platform.   I was a little Methodist girl so I assumed I would probably be the only one, maybe one in a very few people. But as I looked around, I saw many people flooding the altar to be prayed for, and they started lining up shoulder to shoulder from one side of the auditorium to the other.   The altar area was full of people needing a miracle.

I was undaunted.   I knew what I believed. I knew that this was my moment, my destiny to be healed.

I knew this was my time for a miracle and I wasn't leaving without it!   I said to myself, "All these folks can come if they want to, but this miracle is mine tonight."   Brother Hagin started praying for people at my far right, so I just closed my eyes and started focusing on my Savior and Lord. I started rehearsing in my spirit the scriptures I had been meditating on for weeks. When I was ready to receive, I said in my spirit to the Lord, "Father, give me anything and everything You want me to have."

All of a sudden I felt my left leg grow out to be the same length as my right leg! It was instantaneous! I had other things wrong in my body and they were all healed in that moment. I had ulcers in my stomach, healed. I had a twisted pelvis and womb, healed. I had broken my back in this same wreck, and it was healed, too.

I was filled to overflowing with joy and I lifted my hands and began to praise the Lord and thank Him for healing me! Suddenly I began to speak in the most beautiful foreign language I had ever heard. It was just flowing out of me.   I had no idea what was happening but I knew it was the Lord. I continued to speak this amazing fluent language and I began to rationalize what this could mean!

I was going to college the following fall majoring in music at Mississippi State University and one of the college entrance requirements was a foreign language. We didn't have a foreign language at Weir High School.   My mind immediately said, "This is my foreign language! God gave me a foreign language so I can go to college!" I was overjoyed with this new discovery.

I eventually made my way back to my seat with my newly

grown left leg, which now my left pant legs were too short because Mama had hemmed that leg shorter to match my previous length leg!   All could see how much the Lord had lengthened my leg!   I was still speaking in this beautiful foreign language and I was so full of joy!

I finally sat back down in my seat and another altar call was given, for those who wanted to be filled with the Holy Spirit. I had no idea what that meant but if there was more to have from the Lord, then I wanted it!   I jumped up and started trying to get past the ladies and men who had brought me to this momentous service, but my friend, Madelyn Wood, would not let me pass. She was quietly trying to get me to sit back down.

I was trying to be persistent to tell her that if there was more from the Lord then I wanted it, but I could only speak in the foreign language, and she couldn't understand what I was saying!   This went on for a few minutes until finally she said to me, "Honey, you have the Holy Spirit.   That is the language that is coming out of you. It is a sign that you have been filled with the Holy Spirit."

I suddenly remembered the prayer I had prayed at the altar before the Lord touched and healed me. "Lord, give me anything and everything You want me to have." He wanted me to have the Holy Spirit. Even though I had not been introduced to the Holy Spirit yet, I had opened myself up to whatever His will was for me by my submissive prayer. Sometimes God doesn't need us to know everything and be so specific.   He knows what we don't know. He is always looking for our submission, our   willingness to obey whatever He wants. Not my will but Your will be done.

My life was forever changed that night.   I transitioned into the spiritual second stage of my life's journey that evening. I stepped into the active stage of my spiritual walk with Him.

I didn't transition into the final stage, the no more blood stage, the authoritative stage of my life, until our daughter Gabrielle died. I stopped bleeding in my body the day she died. I stepped into my spiritual authority that day.

In Mary's life the final stage of authority was about to begin for her. Mary made a statement to her Son, Jesus. Mary said, "They have no more wine."

In this scripture the wine represents the juice of the grape, or the blood of the grape. This is what comes out when pressed or squeezed. In essence, Mary had chosen to move from the active stage of her life to the authoritative stage of her life. She said to her Messiah Son, "It is time for You to start Your miracle ministry. It is time for You to finish strong." She pushed her Son to the cross that day.

She ultimately said, "I love You, my Son, but I need a Savior more than I need a Son. I have other sons, but there is only one Savior. You are my Messiah. It's time for You to start and finish God's plan for Your life."

When Mary said, "They have no more wine," she was actually making a declaration that she was moving to her next stage of life. She was saying, "I have bled long enough. It's time for You to bleed." I must stop bleeding to step into my authority stage of life. She ultimately said to Jesus, "No more blood!" Mary said I must stop being Your mother and release You to be who You were created to be, not my natural son, but my Savior, my Messiah!

When Mary did this, she stepped into the third and final stage of her life. In the natural we call this menopause, but truly, it is the greatest level of life that can ever be. Whether Mary physically stopped bleeding that day one cannot say, but in her spiritual life she stepped into her authority and it's easy to see by how she spoke to the servants! She spoke with authority when she said, "Whatever He tells you to do, do it!" She spoke from authority that she had earned by her submission to God's plan and will for her life.

Jesus obeyed her that day, and He fulfilled His mission for the final bride. Will you move from where you are to where you were created to be?

Chapter Eight
The Third Day

In the beginning of 2001, our family was on the road in Florida. We did a television show one Saturday afternoon and a scripture was read that caught our attention.

"Come, let us return to the Lord. He has torn us to pieces but He will heal us; He has injured us but He will bind up our wounds. After two days He will revive us; on the third day He will restore us, that we may live in His presence." Hosea 6:1-2 NIV

We immediately wanted to read this passage in the Amplified Bible. *"Come and let us return to the Lord, for He has torn so that He may heal us; He has stricken so that He may bind us up. After two days He will revive us (quicken us, give us life); on the third day He will raise us up that we may live before Him."*

The words in the NIV translation jumped off the page. *"On the third day He will restore us."* We had been shouting

'Restore' for months. We had been prophesying our own future because of a revelation we received. *"But this is a people robbed and plundered; all of them are snared in holes, and they are hidden in prison houses. They are for prey, and no one delivers; for plunder, and no one says, 'Restore!'"* Isaiah 42:22

We received this word just four months before Gabrielle was diagnosed with a brain tumor and given two months to live. We immediately began to speak out of our mouths, "Restore, Restore, Restore!" We knew from studying the entire passage that Israel had stayed in the condition that they were in because no one would prophesy or even say, "Restore!" So, the opposite of that must be true. If only someone would have said, "Restore!" then Israel could have been changed, saved, and RESTORED!

We took this revelation to heart in our lives. We talked "Restore!" We sang, "Restore!" We prayed, "Restore!" We did not stop. We continued. We believed for eleven months for restoration to be in Gabrielle's body and in our family. On Nov. 23, 1999 Gabrielle left this earth and moved to heaven.

There are no words to tell you how we felt, and I don't have enough space to share it all. That's why we wrote two books dedicated specifically to Gabrielle and the time we went through with her, the grief, and recovery afterwards. It is life changing beyond anything anyone can ever imagine. If you need these books please contact our ministry and we will get them to you, or you can order them directly from our ministry web site.

We were broken.   We were bleeding out spiritually. We were treated by many in the Christian world like we had leprosy, and we were unclean.   They weren't thinking anything we didn't feel. We felt like the biggest failures in the universe.   We didn't know what we had done wrong. Surely, we had done something very wrong for our daughter to die and we were fully engaged in our faith!   We never doubted for a moment and yet, she still died.   All I could do was lift up my broken heart to the Lord and say, "Will you restore us now?"

He did, but it took time, much time of pressing in, time of dying to self, time of refusing to let go *'until you bless me'* (Genesis 32:26).   We desired restoration, but it was more than a desire.   If God did not restore us we could not go on. We would die without restoration and we knew it!

We were hungering and thirsting for restoration.   We preached it.   We talked about it.   It was in every conversation. We must have restoration!   After months and months of this prophetic word Harry turned to me one day and said, "What's next?   There must be something after restoration."

I didn't have an answer.   We were getting bits and pieces of the restoration puzzle in our lives.   We were literally surviving on the revelations we received from the Lord, but Harry was right.   What is next?   There must be something else!

Not too many days later we were preaching in California on a Sunday morning.   We entered the church and headed to the office to get ready for service.   As we did the pastor came into the office with a yellow sticky notepaper in his hand.   He said, "The Lord gave me a word in the car coming to church this morning."

We both said, "What did He say?"

The pastor read his note, "After restoration comes divine visitation."

You could have knocked us over with a feather! We had been asking God, "What's next? What is after restoration?" God answered! AFTER RESTORATION COMES DIVINE VISITATION!

Just so you can see the timeline that we were living on, this happened in August of 2000, just nine months after Gabrielle had gone to heaven. We continued to look for what this word could mean. It became more clear when we read the following scripture.

"So, I will restore to you the years that the swarming locust has eaten, the crawling locust, the consuming locust, and the chewing locust, My great army which I sent among you. You shall eat in plenty and be satisfied, and praise the name of the LORD your God, Who has dealt wondrously with you; and My people shall never be put to shame. Then you shall know that I am in the midst of Israel: I am the LORD your God and there is no other. My people shall never be put to shame. And it shall come to pass afterward that I will pour out My Spirit on all flesh; your sons and your daughters shall prophesy, your old men shall dream dreams, your young men shall see visions. And also on My menservants and on My maidservants I will pour out My Spirit in those days. And I will show wonders in the heavens and in the earth: blood and fire and pillars of smoke. The sun shall be turned into darkness, and the moon into blood, before the coming of the great and awesome day of the LORD. And it shall come to pass that whoever calls on the name of the LORD shall be saved. For in Mount Zion and in Jerusalem there shall be deliverance, as the LORD has said, among the remnant whom the LORD calls." Joel 2:25-32.

God said that He will RESTORE! He will restore the years! He will restore what is taken, what is eaten, what is devoured! He will restore!

Harry and I already had revelation of restoration. This scripture just confirmed it more to us! But what we really noticed was in verse 28 that God says, *"And afterward."*

After what?

After restoration! God will pour out His Spirit upon all flesh after restoration! What is after restoration for us? God will pour out His Spirit upon us, upon all our flesh; after restoration comes divine visitation! We got it!

So, you can see when the scripture was read out of Hosea 6:1,2 that talked of restoration on the third day, we had to find out more about the third day. When is the third day? Is that a day? Is that a time period? Of course, the first third day that comes to all Christian's minds is on the third day Jesus rose from the grave! He rose from the dead and He lives today! We began to look up every third day scripture we could find and there are many!

The first one is in the first chapter of Genesis! That is only the beginning! There are third day references throughout the scripture. The third day had something to do with the season we were in at that moment! We studied, we searched, we prayed, and God revealed. It became apparent that the beginning of 2000 was the start of the third day on God's timetable.

But how did we get this? The timeline that we are in began with our Lord and Savior Jesus Christ. His life, death, and resurrection began the number system of the time that we live.

0 AD until Dec. 31, 999 was the first day.

How did I get that? With God a day is as a thousand years and a thousand years is as a day. The Bible says this in both the Old Testament in Psalm 90:4 and also, in the New Testament in II Peter 3:8.

With this revelation then the timeline would look like this.
Jan. 1, 0 AD ________________________________Dec. 31, 999
first day

Jan. 1, 1000________________________________Dec.31, 1999
second day

Jan. 1, 2000 began the third day on God's timetable. We are in the midst of the third day right now.

We were not looking for this date to be a red-letter day on earth! No, we were watching and waiting to see what would happen with technology! Y2K was prophesied to be disastrous and people were focused on it. Satan had the entire world focused on the wrong thing! This December 31, 1999 was the end of the second day.

And did anything happen with technology? Nothing, absolutely nothing! Nothing happened at all! So, we didn't even suspect that God had a day that should be noticed, a time in history when the second day and all that was ordained and destined for that time period was over, the second day ended. No one seemed to notice. The great thing with God about a period of time being over is that another one is beginning! As quickly as the second day ended the third day began. The third day, the bride's day, the resurrection day of God's people and the fulfillment of God's plan began January 1, 2000, the third day.

We cannot miss what was ordained and destined for the third day. We began to look at scripture after scripture that referred to the third day. There are so many, and they are all relevant to the time in history that we are living right now! I won't begin to take you to every 'third day' scripture. I will leave this up to you to 'dig' and find out for yourself. But I do want to point out the story in I Samuel 30 because it deals with another dimension of the third day: Recovery.

"Now it happened, when David and his men came to Ziklag, on the third day, that the Amalekites had invaded the South and Ziklag, attacked Ziklag and burned it with fire, and had taken captive the women and those who were there, from small to great; they did not kill anyone, but carried them away and went their way. So David and his men came to the city, and there it was, burned with fire; and their wives, their sons, and their daughters had been taken captive. Then David and the people who were with him lifted up their voices and wept, until they had no more power to weep. And David's two wives, Ahinoam the Jezreelitess, and Abigail the widow of Nabal the Carmelite, had been taken captive. Now David was greatly distressed, for the people spoke of stoning him, because the soul of all the people was grieved, every man for his sons and his daughters. But David strengthened himself in the LORD his God. Then David said to Abiathar the priest, Ahimelech's son, 'Please bring the ephod here to me.' And Abiathar brought the ephod to David. So David inquired of the LORD, saying, 'Shall I pursue this troop? Shall I overtake them?' And He answered him, 'Pursue, for you shall surely overtake them and without fail recover all.'"
1 Samuel 30:1-9.

No matter how much you feel you have lost in the journey called life, God has an ultimate plan for restoration and recovery in this very season of time in which we find ourselves. This third day season is to strengthen your faith to believe God once again for restoration and recovery of all that the enemy has stolen. It's time to make the thief bring it all back times seven! Be refreshed and renewed. Be revived, restored and recovered. It's time. It's time.

Chapter Nine
Don't Look Back

Let's look again at this, *"He who touches the dead body of any person shall be unclean for seven days. He shall purify himself with the water for impurity [made with the ashes of the burned heifer] on the third day, and on the seventh day he shall be clean. But if he does not purify himself the third day, then the seventh day he shall not be clean."* Numbers 19:11-12.

Are you thinking, "What has this got to do with me?"

Let's read on and I will show you. *"Whoever touches the corpse of any who has died and does not purify himself defiles the tabernacle of the Lord, and that person shall be cut off from Israel. Because the water for impurity was not sprinkled upon him, he shall be unclean; his uncleanness is still upon him."* Numbers 19:13.

The first thing I want you to notice is that this scripture is talking about the third and seventh days. This reference makes it applicable to you and me as the resurrected and finished bride of Christ.

As you are reading you are probably already connecting the reference to 'purify himself' with the time for purification. God is setting us up in this day, the third day, to have the choice to purify ourselves. He is not forcing purification on us. In fact, it cannot be anyone else's choice. We must choose to purify ourselves. We must choose to be the righteousness of God. We must choose to yield our instruments (voices and sounds) to righteousness and not to wickedness. All day, every day, it's always going to be my choice and ultimately yours too.

How is this possible? How can we purify ourselves? In the area of purification for our sins we can't purify ourselves. Only through the blood of the pure and blameless Lamb of God, who takes away the sins of the world, Jesus, can we be cleansed in the spirit.

So why would the Bible say to purify ourselves? Look at the prior verse, "He who touches the dead body of any person shall be unclean." This is what the Holy Spirit illuminated my eyes to see. For many years I have been ministering in the area of letting go of the past. I have preached, taught, and sang this phrase! When driving down the road of life, rip off the rearview mirror!

We have preached many messages on it, we have written several books on the topic, but I have never seen, until now, that on the third day God had ordained and predestined this time as THE TIME to let go of those things behind us that are keeping us from moving forward! There has never been a time more appropriate to turn loose of your past and run into your future than this!

I saw it. God revealed it. 'He who touches the dead body of any person . . .' How could that be today? I might not have been able to see what this meant had our daughter, Gabrielle, still been here with us.   When the scripture said the body of any person, the dead body of any person, it is in reference to our pasts.

After she went to heaven, I was still struggling months later. The image of her little sick body continued to torment us both day and night. The questions, unanswered, the past vision that played over and over in our minds was almost more than either of us could bear. One morning I was sitting in my prayer chair in the kitchen and I couldn't take it any more. I cried out to God to help me. I said to Him, "What am I supposed to be feeling? What am I supposed to be seeing in my mind? Help me, Lord!"

At that moment the Holy Spirit spoke to me and He said, **"Gabrielle is not in your past, but she is in your future."**

That one statement hit my spirit with the full force of the universe! I got it! Gabrielle is not dead. She is not behind me. She is not in the grave.

She is not in the cemetery. SHE IS ALIVE! SHE IS IN FRONT OF ME! SHE IS IN MY FUTURE! I began to get a new vision, not of her sick and dying, but of her well, whole happy, living. LIVING!!!

Now with that revelation in your mind and hopefully, in your heart, can you see what God was saying in Numbers 19 to us about the third day? How can we purify ourselves? We can purify ourselves by turning loose of our pasts, by turning loose of those things behind us that have tormented us and kept us from moving forward, by turning loose of those things that have frozen and paralyzed us with fear.

We have been deceived into thinking that if we don't think about those people who have gone on to heaven, we are dishonoring them. Nothing could be further from the truth. You can't stop thinking about them! We can think about them. But we must not think about them as if they are behind us. We must not cling to them! We must only cling to Him! We must think about them in front of us, ahead of us, alive and well, in our future.

We don't generally do this though. We rehearse memories of the way they were before. We don't allow the Holy Spirit to give us a new vision, a fresh vision, a true vision. We talk of people who have gone to heaven as if they don't exist anymore. We say things like, "She WAS so sweet. She LOOKED like me." We talk about them in the past tense. We don't talk about them in the present tense and the future tense because we have no vision of the present and the future. We have only looked back!

By thinking of Gabrielle only behind me, I am stating with my mind that I don't believe that she is in front of me. By looking behind me, looking for her behind me, I am searching behind me for something that is alive. You and I both know that there is nothing behind us that is alive. Everything, even one minute ago, is our past. Everything in the past is dead. It is already in the grave. It has already begun to stink!

When we won't turn loose of those things behind us, we are paralyzed with fear. Our past predicts our future. It reminds me of the story in the Bible about Lot and his family. Angels came and got the family out of Sodom before the destroying angels hit the city with a destroying fire. They were warned, *"When they had brought them outside [one of the angels] said, 'Escape for your life! Do not look behind you, or stop anywhere in the entire valley.'"* Genesis 19:17 AMP.

The angels told them not to look back! Then a few verses later in verse 22, *"They were warned again, 'Hurry and take refuge there.'"*

God will always make a way of escape if we will only heed His words. But Lot's wife just could not keep from looking back. *"But Lot's wife, from behind him, [foolishly, longingly] looked [back toward Sodom in an act of disobedience], and she turned into a pillar of salt."* Genesis 19:26 AMP. Lot's wife was chosen along with the rest of her family to escape the punishment of the city. She was chosen to be a part of the next move of God. But she would not obey the command to not look back.

Instead of being a part of God's next big move, she became a monument to the past. She became a monument to her 'last accomplishment.' Don't be like Lot's wife. Choose to turn loose of the past and let it go. Choose to move with the Spirit of God into the next big position of His power and presense. Don't get caught in thought. Don't get caught rehearsing the past and lose your eternal future perspective.

The Holy Spirit has warned many of us time and time again. He has so softly warned, "Don't look back. There is nothing behind you of any value to your future." And yet so many are guilty of holding on to the past. We tend to continually look behind; meditating on the things of the past, rehearsing the 'what if's' the 'would of' 'should of' 'could of' of our minds.

These places of the mind will keep you in captivity, a prison, of questions. These walls that are built of our own doing are what God was warning us of in scripture. When He said *"He who touches the dead body."* Numbers 19:11.

Anything behind you, anything in your memories whether pleasant or horrible, are in the past. They are behind you and they are DEAD! If you keep dragging these old corpses around with you, you will begin to smell like dead things.

What is a dead thing? It is a decaying, stinking, rotten, lifeless object. Anything dead cannot be of any value to anyone's future! But many people continue to drag this stinking mass around with them. It is in their conversation, their thoughts, and their actions.

God is telling us to 'purify ourselves' and leave the dead things behind. It is no wonder that no one wants to hang around with or be friends with people who won't let go of the past. They stink! They smell like death, decay! God said to purify ourselves. Turning loose of the past is a one-man job. Only I can do it. You can't help me or make me.

If we choose not to obey Him, then God's Word says that we are unclean because of our choice! In fact, in verse 13 it reads, *"Whoever touches the corpse of any who has died and does not purify himself DEFILES the tabernacle of the Lord."*

Who is the tabernacle of the Lord? We are supposed to be God's tabernacle, His dwelling place! The rest of that verse 13 states, *"Because the water for impurity was not sprinkled upon him, he shall be unclean; his uncleanness is still upon him."*

Don't miss that the verb is present tense. *"His uncleanness IS STILL upon him."*

Oh, how sad to think that those who will not let it go, and turn it loose, ARE STILL unclean. Jesus came, He was sent by God to take away the sins of the world. When we refuse to turn loose of the past, the dead things that control our future, we are stating that we do not accept what Jesus did on the cross for us!

I will receive, I choose to receive all that God has ordained and destined for me. I will not refuse anything that Jesus has done for me. Therefore, I must receive the ability, not in my own strength, but in Jesus' strength, to let go of all things behind me. This reads so beautifully in the Amplified Bible, *"Jesus said to him, 'No one who puts his hand to the plow and looks back [to the things behind] is fit for the kingdom of God.'"* Luke 9:62 AMP

That just about sums it up. That is a strong scripture and it is very plain. Jesus said that looking back will make you unfit for the kingdom of God! Don't forget what Paul said in Philippians. *"But one thing I do [it is my one aspiration]: forgetting what lies behind and straining forward to what lies ahead I press toward the goal to win the [supreme and heavenly] prize to which God in Christ Jesus is calling us upward."* Philippians 3:13-14 AMP

Many people have preached messages from this passage, but I have never heard anyone emphasize what the Holy Spirit emphasized to me. What was the one thing that Paul aspired to do in his life? He chose to forget what lies behind. Leave the past in the past. This one thing that Paul, the great apostle, did was to forget the past! Don't feel bad! You are not alone. Even Paul had to forget the past before he could press forward!

In the many years that I have been in ministry I have never seen anyone turned to a pillar of salt immediately as Lot's wife was when she disobeyed God's command and looked back. But I do know people who have refused to get a new vision in front of them. They continue to look back. It is in every area of their lives. As you watch them you see them slowly dry up. They lose their love for life. They lose their health.

Their bones become brittle. They become bitter about

everything. Many times, their gall bladder doesn't function properly. They lose all that is dear to them. Everything begins to die around them, because death breeds death. A stagnant pond will cause sickness, disease, and yes, even death. They eventually become a pillar of salt. They eventually become a monument to the past instead of a bright beacon of hope for the future.

Bitterness comes out of unanswered questions and unresolved emotional issues. There is a common symbol in the pre-Babylonian, syrophonecian Hebrew language within every question word. There are only six question words. You already know them. They are the same in every language.

Who
What
When
Where
Why
How

Six questions can stop you in your life's journey and keep you looking back at your past. Six is the number for flesh. Our flesh cries out for answers to these questions.

When we are in tune with the Spirit of God our flesh will still cry out. Our God is not flesh. He is Spirit and Truth. He answers in Spirit and in Truth. He will never satisfy our flesh. Our flesh can cry out for all of its existence but our God who is not flesh will never make our flesh feel 'satisfied'. We must get out of our flesh questions by our own choice to turn it loose, let it go, forgive and forget so to speak.

There is one common symbol in the ancient Hebrew

language in the six 'question' words. It's the symbol for chaos. Within the question words chaos can be presented. Unanswered questions can release the power of chaos in our lives and eventually into our bodies as well.

Bitterness comes out of us; it shows up in our emotional realm. It surfaces in our thoughts, our speech, and even in our flesh. When we have unresolved questions in our minds that eventually become unresolved issues of our hearts, we can become sick in our bodies because of it. Bitterness will take root if it is not pulled up.

I believe that is why I became ill with colon cancer after the death of our precious six-year-old daughter Gabrielle. I felt that God was not answering my heart questions. I felt that He was leaving me hanging, not satisfying my needs. I felt that God broke covenant with me. I felt that He was cruel and that if He really loved me, He would have done what I asked and healed our daughter. Did you notice how many times I said, "I felt?" I was being driven by my feelings instead of my spirit.

I would not let myself, even to my own mind, think or say these feelings, so I suppressed my heart cries. I stuffed them deep in my heart; hoping to never have to look at them, never have to deal with them. It was not many months until this type of unresolved hurt became cancerous to my flesh.

Even while Gabrielle was still on the earth, I began to have problems with my intestines. I was uncomfortable, nauseous, a bitter taste in my mouth. I lost my appetite; I was falling deep into depression. But I could not let anyone see this, not even my own self! So, I stuffed all my feelings deep, so deep that they surfaced in my colon!

A week after Gabrielle went to heaven I began to throw up. I would wake up very violently sick, and vomit until it passed. Each time it took about three hours to stop throwing up, every 10 to 15 minutes for three hours. Then I would be very nauseous for another three hours and then I would feel better again. This would happen every few days. For three months this went on and on.

When Harry and I consulted with friends who were doctors they all seemed to agree that this was just my body reacting to the grief. When Gabrielle went to heaven, I felt that my flesh had been ripped apart and this was just the reaction to the ripped feeling I had in my soul.

No matter what was prescribed by the doctors to help me through this, there was nothing that made it better, and nothing made it stop. It just continued day after day, week after week, month after month. Three months to the day of Gabrielle going to heaven they diagnosed me with colon cancer and did surgery immediately.

I didn't want to live. I didn't want to stay here. I thought this was a good way to leave the earth and go and be with Jesus and Gabrielle. The Father God had other plans. They were revealed to me as I was being wheeled into surgery.

They had already prepped me and had given me a sedative. Harry was beside me all the way, holding my hand, praying over me. I had made my decision. I was leaving this earth and not looking back. Just as I was being pushed through the surgery doors I was suddenly caught up to heaven. I was standing before the Lord. I wanted Him to say the two words my heart longed to hear from Him. My spirit was silently pleading with Him to say, "Well done." "Come on, say it," I silently pleaded with Him. Finally, He spoke. He said to me, "You have always wanted to stand before me and hear two words, "Well done."

The Lord said to me, "If you come home now and stand

before Me, you will not hear two words. You will only hear one word." And then He said it. "Well?" His voice inflection went higher at the end as He asked me the question, "Well?"

My mind was reeling. I was screaming, "What?"

I began to digest what the Spirit of God was saying to me. As I did so, the Lord continued to speak. He said, "I want you to stand before Me but not now. I have not called you home yet. You are not finished and if you come now you will be in direct disobedience to My will for your life."

As badly as I wanted to escape the pain of this earth, as badly as I wanted to leave here and go be with Gabrielle, I would never be willfully disobedient to God's will and He knew that.

As I focused on His face and felt the peace and warmth of His presense, I thought for a moment and then I said to Him, "Lord, I will go back and complete what You have for me, but I want three things. I want my health restored. I want my family restored. And I want our joy restored."

There was no hesitation at all from the Lord. He simply and powerfully said, "Done." It was as if the electricity of the paddles had hit me! His word, "Done!" was so powerful to my spirit and body that Harry said even under sedation I spoke to him.

I was back in my sedated body being wheeled into surgery. My precious husband knows me so well. He knew that I didn't want to stay here. He knew that I had made a choice to die, to get out of the pain of this world.

As they were wheeling me through the surgery doors Harry was leaning over me. With parted lips that were about to speak the most unselfish words on the earth, for he had already decided to release me if I wanted to go. He had already decided to tell me that if I saw Jesus or if I saw Gabrielle and if I wanted to go on that he and the boys would be all right.

Just as he leaned over me to speak these words, Harry said that I opened one eye. And even under the medication, the sedation, I spoke to him and said, "I'm not leaving you."

Harry told me later that at that moment he knew that I would be all right. He knew that I would live, because I had chosen to live. He knew that I had made my decision that somehow, I had dealt with the pain of my heart and had chosen to stay and fight the battle with him.

It was a long and hard physical, emotional, mental, and spiritual battle back to the restored position that God sealed and settled in His presense with the words, "Done." But it has been worth it. The growth in both of us, the power of choice that has been revealed to us through this journey cannot be undone forever within us. The fire of the journey has brought change inside of us. We are simply 'His.' And that's enough.

It's not instant, nor is it magic. It is not some fairy dust that is sprinkled over you and you wake up restored. It is not even something you can pick up at the altar of a church or have someone lay hands on you and pray for this. There is not enough oil in the world poured over your head that can bring this to fruition.

This place in God can only be attained through the fire of God, the testing and trials, the troubles and situations, the circumstances that we all wish we never had to experience. It is there for the taking, this place of purification, but we must willingly embrace it, receive it, die in it, and come out refined and purified as His resurrected bride.

Chapter Ten

Life Produces Life

The seed of life can only produce life. The seed of death can only produce death. Seed will always produce after its own kind. *"Because the water for impurity was not sprinkled upon them."* Numbers 19:13. What does the Bible call the Word of God? The Bible relates water with His Word. *"So that He might sanctify her, having cleansed her by the washing of WATER WITH THE WORD."* Ephesians 5:26

The water for impurity for our lives is God's Word. It can wash us as white as snow. It can bring life to a lifeless soul. It can bring life to a sick and diseased body. It can take away the sins of the world when the *'Word became flesh and dwelt among us,'* in the form of Jesus.

The Word of God is the water for which we thirst. We cannot neglect the reading, washing and cleansing time in our lives. We must never allow the enemy to get us to a place where we dry up from a lack of water of the Word. We cannot live in our physical bodies without water. When we begin to dehydrate our flesh starts to break down. We can go for many days without food, but we cannot survive without water!

Don't try and make your spiritual body do the impossible. It cannot survive without the water of the Word to keep your spirit hydrated. Don't forget that. *"And whoever shall call on the name of the Lord shall be delivered and saved, for in Mount Zion and in Jerusalem there shall be those who escape, as the Lord has said, and among the remnant [of survivors] shall be those whom the Lord calls."* Joel 2:32 AMP.

When a person complains to me that they are 'so spiritually dry,' without meaning to, they have revealed to me that they are not in God's Word. His Word is refreshing to our souls and spirits. His Word brings hope and healing when nothing else can. His Word is His water to quench our thirsty souls. If you are thirsty it's because you stopped drinking from the well. Don't complain about your condition if you are not willing to drink from His Word that will water you!

The American definition of remnant is the throw away, the piece of carpet that we use to wipe our feet on, the piece of fabric that becomes the dishrag or the dust cloth. But God calls the remnant a survivor. I am God's survivor, are you? You are not a throw away piece of fabric or carpet. You are a survivor and He calls from the remnant of survivors.

I hope you see that remnant means a small group of those who have overcome trials, troubles, and situations. This is a small group of survivors. I looked it up in the Hebrew and remnant really means survivors! God is looking for those who will survive. He is looking for the ones who will not give up, who will continue to press on, push through, never give up, and never stop!

And from this group the Bible says, is the group from

whom the Lord calls! His calling is not for the one who has nevergone through anything. He does not call from the group whose life has been a 'tiptoe through the tulips!' He calls from those who have survived the war of life, the holocaust of the spirit of antichrist! God is calling you!

"But he who endures to the end will be saved." Matthew 24:13.

Endurance, remnant, survivor, these are words the Lord has carefully put within His Word so we don't become confused about life's journey. The stages of life are vital, and the transitions are difficult. It takes endurance, a pushing, pulling, contracting, and birthing of who you are on the inside to become who the Lord created you to be. You are in the remnant, but will you be called? Show Him every day that you are not just a survivor, but also an overcomer. For what you don't overcome, will overcome you.

I refuse to say that I am a cancer survivor. Why? I have done much more than survive cancer. I have overcome it. I have been diagnosed and come through colon cancer twice, seven years apart. Then my colon twisted, and I survived and overcame that death experience. I have had skin cancer on my face twice! I have survived and overcome it. What is the difference between a survivor and an overcomer? Fear.

I am not afraid of cancer. In fact, I have said so many times, cancer, cancer, cancer I am not afraid of you. I refuse to respect, honor, or revere anything other than our Lord and Savior. Fear is defined as respect, honor, and reverence.

I will only fear my Lord. I will not give a moment's attention to cancer. I will not fear it or fear its return. In the beginning of my journey with cancer I was a survivor, but now, after twenty years of battling that devilish disease, I have overcome it. I am an overcomer.

I am more than a conqueror through Christ! *"In all these things we are more than conquerors through Him that loved us."* Romans 8:37. Yes, in all these things I am more than a conqueror, because Christ has overcome, and I get to enjoy the journey of an overcomer inside of my identity in Christ!

Life is just four little letters, but the center two letters really give the full explanation of life. I-F. This little word inside of a word 'if' really tells us that life in itself is a choice. I can choose which way to go. It is my choice. I can choose if I go this way, or if I go that way. My life is about the 'ifs'. What do I choose to do, and which way do I choose to go?

"But if serving the LORD seems undesirable to you, then choose for yourselves this day whom you will serve, whether the gods your ancestors served beyond the Euphrates, or the gods of the Amorites, in whose land you are living. But as for me and my household, we will serve the LORD." Joshua 24:15 NIV.

My life seeds of choice produce life. When I choose for my future and the future of my family the things that produce eternal life, right choices, good choices, that reflect a wisdom thought pattern instead of an instant gratification thought pattern, then the seeds of life are planted into the fertile grounds of my future. Eventually, if I won't faint and give up, these seeds will produce after their own kind.

Once I have planted my life seeds, then I have the choice of how much water is given to them through the water of the Word of God. I make good life choices and plant those life seeds for my future, and then I water them every day through His Word to bring about the full and complete harvest within each seed.

Eventually, the harvest of life will come up and produce the fruit necessary to sustain me until I cross over to the other side with Jesus, which is also produced by my life choices of seed while I am here on this little trip of time.   As I journey from my passive stage, through my active stage, and transition into my authoritative stage of life, the seed planting, time watering, and harvesting continue on and on!

This tiny measure of time in a great expanse of eternity is what we hold so dear, so precious.   We cling to it as if it is all we get!   But this is only the 'womb of heaven' experience if you will. This is only the natural forty weeks of development inside the womb of your mother with an earthly lifetime to follow once the pushing and pressing have brought forth the birthing of yet another 'life' to live.

Would we ever long to go back to the womb?   Would we even consider that as the most important time of our lives? And yet, when we hold so tightly the short expanse of time we call this earthly life as if that is all there will ever be, we are saying that the 'womb of heaven' experience on the earth that is necessary to birth us into the heavenly life that is set before us, is the most important time. We are saying that this earth experience, this womb experience of development time, is what 'life' is all about instead of what is to come. Eternal life is just that, infinite eternal life! The Bible calls our earth experience a vapor in comparison with our eternal time.

Let's talk about how we can truly be ready for eternity. How can I be sure I have done what I need to do, made the right choices to be ready to be His bride without spot or wrinkle?   What can I do? Let's talk about the purifying process necessary to produce His image within us.

Let's talk about His Holy Spirit fire that is upon our heads and takes over our tongues and mouths once the Holy Spirit moves inside this temple. Do you not know that your body is the temple of the Holy Ghost? *"Do you not know that your body is the temple (the very sanctuary) of the Holy Spirit Who lives within you, Whom you have received [as a Gift] from God?"* I Corinthians 6:19 AMPC.

"When suddenly there came a sound from heaven like the rushing of a violent tempest blast, and it filled the whole house in which they were sitting. And there appeared to them tongues resembling fire, which were separated and distributed and which settled on each one of them. And they were all filled (diffused throughout their souls) with the Holy Spirit and began to speak in other (different, foreign) languages (tongues), as the Spirit kept giving them clear and loud expression [in each tongue in appropriate words]." Acts 2:2-4 APMC.

Receiving the infilling of the Holy Spirit is a separate experience from your salvation experience. Jesus told the disciples, *"And I will ask the Father, and He will give you another Comforter (Counselor, Helper, Intercessor, Advocate, Strengthener, and Standby), that He may remain with you forever- The Spirit of Truth, Whom the world cannot receive (welcome, take to its heart), because it does not see Him or know and recognize Him. But you know and recognize Him, for He lives with you [constantly] and will be in you."* John 14: 16-17 AMPC.

The Holy Spirit was promised by Jesus to be sent to take His place with them. And Jesus so beautifully explained to them that they have the Holy Spirit with them already, but soon He will be IN YOU! This is a separate experience of an infilling of the Holy Spirit when He moves from the outside of being 'with us' to the inside of being 'in us!' The Holy Spirit lives inside of you when you invite Him to move into and possess your soul and spirit. You become the very temple of the Holy Spirit.

When Paul was doing his evangelistic traveling ministry he came through the upper inland districts and came down to Ephesus. He found some disciples of Jesus there who were following and worshiping the Lord. They had given their hearts and lives to the Lord. Paul asked them a beautiful question in Acts.

"And he asked them, 'Did you receive the Holy Spirit when you believed [on Jesus as the Christ]?' And they said 'No, we have not even heard that there is a Holy Spirit.' Paul asked, 'Into what [baptism] then were you baptized?' They said, 'Into John's baptism.' And Paul said, 'John baptized with the baptism of repentance, continually telling the people that they should believe in the One Who was to come after him, that is, in Jesus [having a conviction full of joyful trust that He is Christ, the Messiah, and being obedient to Him].' On hearing this they were baptized [again, this time] in the name of the Lord Jesus. And as Paul laid his hands upon them, the Holy Spirit came on them, and they spoke in [foreign, unknown] tongues (languages) and prophesied." Acts 19:2-6 AMPC.

There is a fire, a purifying fire that must burn within us continually if we are to be made ready, and then continue to stay ready for the return of our Lord. From studying the scriptures in both the New Testament and the Old Testament I have named this holy process of God's fire.

PURI-FIRE

Take a look with me in the scripture. *"Now stay outside of the camp for seven days, all of you who have killed anyone or touched a dead body. Then purify yourselves and your captives on the third and seventh days. Remember also to purify all your garments and everything made of leather, goat's hair, or wood." Then Eleazar the priest said to the men who were in the battle, "This is the commandment*

Jehovah has given Moses: 'Anything that will stand heat-such as gold, silver, bronze, iron, tin, or lead, shall be passed through fire in order to be made ceremonially pure; it must then be further purified with the purification water. But anything that won't stand heat shall be purified by the water alone. On the seventh day you must wash your clothes and be purified, and then you may come back into the camp."
Numbers 31:19-24 TLB.

God desires for His bride to be ready for His coming. He will not come back for a bride with spots and wrinkles. He promises that she must be prepared and found ready. Nor does He want a bride that is immature and still in kindergarten!

We must take the correction and preparation times of our lives to grow up spiritually. We must not continue to go through hard times and never change. In fact, some people go through difficult situations and instead of maturing, being made ready for His coming, they just get hard, bitter, and calloused, still focusing on themselves, continuing to think that every little thing in the world is about them!

We must get over this type of childlike and immature thinking. We must tell ourselves each and every day, "It's not about me; it's not about what I want. It's about Him, my Savior, my Messiah, my Bridegroom, Jesus! It's about what He wants, He desires, and what delights Him!"

Ultimately, when we are one with Jesus, and our lives are completely and totally sold out to His will, then when our hearts are toward pleasing Him we are saturated with satisfaction. My pleasure is His pleasure!

When I researched the definitions of the meanings of the numbers 3 and 7, I found that 3 is feminine and 7 is masculine in their nature.

On the seventh day God said, "It is finished." The last three words of Jesus as He was dying on the cross were "It is finished." In the last chapter of Revelation, you find that the bride must say, "It is finished," to bring about the complete circle, the circle of threes to bring about the fulfilled completion.

It is finished. (Father said.)
It is finished. (Bridegroom said.)
It is finished. (Bride must say.)

Strong's OT: 7992 Sheliyshiy (shel-ee-shee'); ordinal from OT: 7969; third; feminine a third (part); by extension, a third (day, year or time); specifically, a third-story cell):

KJV - third (part, rank, time), three (years old).

Strong's OT: 7651 Sheba` (sheh'-bah); or (masculine) shib`ah (shib-aw'); from OT: 7650; a primitive cardinal number; seven (as the sacred full one); also (adverbially) seven times; by implication, a week; by extension, an indefinite number:

KJV - (+by) seven [-folds], [-teen, -teenth], -th, times). Compare OT: 7658.

(Biblesoft's New Exhaustive Strong's Numbers and Concordance with Expanded Greek-Hebrew Dictionary. Copyright © 1994, 2003 Biblesoft, Inc. and International Bible Translators, Inc.)

You can see several definitions for third and seventh. The point I want you to notice in this instance is that the third is feminine and seventh is masculine.

It's truly up to us, to you and me, what we choose to allow to rule our lives. I can choose to allow the Holy Spirit to retrain me to think like He thinks, or I can continue to let the enemy's planted thoughts destroy my future. I can choose to not allow old memories to rule my future. I can choose to walk in forgiveness and not allow what others have done to me to take root within my physical life and heart.

In the ancient Hebrew language, the word 'repent' means to burn the house to the ground as if it never existed. That seems like an odd definition until you understand in the ancient language words had more than a simple definition. Each word had a story that went with it to explain the full meaning. In the case of the word 'repent' the story went like this.

Picture a scene where one city was opposing another city. There was a war between them. There was a war between two sides, and one side conquered the other side. The conquering side took the captives, literally everyone and everything on the losing side, and marched them away from their homes.

They marched all the captives far away from their city. Once they were removed far enough away from their homes but still within their eyesight, they turned all the conquered people back and made them watch as the conquerors burned everything to the ground, leaving those who were conquered nothing behind them to long to return.

Thus, the word 'repent' has the meaning of burning your past to the ground as if it never existed leaving you nowhere to long to go back. Ultimately, it is what the Lord asks of us when we trust Him with our lives and future.

Isaiah 43:18-19 gives us a good word picture of this word 'repent' in the wording to forget those things which lie behind. Don't remember those things that are behind. Don't remember or rehearse your past over and over. Forget it. Don't think about it. You no longer have a past to return to, you are forever focusing forward.

When we truly repent before the Lord, we can turn loose of every emotion connected to our past memories and allow the Lord to heal us completely. It's not that we have spiritual amnesia. That's not it at all. We have memories, but those emotional scars that once accompanied the memories can be released. We can actually remember without the pain associated with the memory. We can have full memory without the 'painful memories.'

I can remember the car wreck on May 4, 1968 without it tearing me up inside every time I think about it now. That took a long time to get to this place, but I kept taking every thought captive, and casting down every imagination, over and over again.

I can remember Gabrielle going to heaven without the rivers of tears that once flooded my life with every tiny memory. Forgiveness creates a place in our memories that allows us to turn loose of the pain of the past without the removal of the past. The past is just that. It's the past. But it shouldn't be the present, after time has gone by. We should learn to live in the present without the pain of the past haunting our every thought.

Chapter Eleven
Pay Attention to the Numbers

There are so many scriptures that deal with purification and the waiting process.   We cannot be purified without the process of purification. It will never happen instantly. It is a process that must be applied to our lives for as long as it takes to bring about the desired outcome.   There is not enough natural oil on our heads, or enough fairy dust that will do for us what the puri-fire can and will do for us.

There are specific numbers that continue to be revealed when dealing with the process of purification, three and seven specifically.   Then there are other numbers used for identification of certain distinctions.   Notice the numbers as the scriptures unveil before you as you read.

Earlier we discussed the following scripture at one level. Let's look at it again a little deeper. This is definitely a part of the purification process for humanity here on the earth, but don't miss what the Spirit is saying. Don't just see words and miss the Holy Spirit's point.

The Bible, every word of it, is written by divine inspiration, and is timeless. Therefore, what we thought might have been done away with, or fulfilled, or under the law, when we look with the eyes of the Spirit of God, we see a word that applies directly to us, right now! (He who has eyes to see and ears to hear, let him see and hear what the Spirit is saying.)

"A woman who becomes pregnant and gives birth to a son will be ceremonially unclean for seven days, just as she is unclean during her monthly period. On the eighth day the boy is to be circumcised. Then the woman must wait thirty-three days to be purified from her bleeding. She must not touch anything sacred or go to the sanctuary until the days of her purification are over. If she gives birth to a daughter, for two weeks (fourteen days) the woman will be unclean, as during her period. Then she must wait sixty-six days to be purified from her bleeding." Leviticus 12:2-5 NIV.

Blood is a vital part of purification. That is why the blood of Jesus had to be shed. He had to be pierced and His blood flow for our sins. There are some specific points we need to look at together. Notice there is a different time period for purification for male babies than there is for female babies.

The time frame is exactly twice as long for the female as it is for the male. Don't get all 'down on women' now and say to yourself, "I knew it! Women are twice as bad as men!" This is not what it is saying at all!

Notice that, as all things throughout this book, we see things in three stages. In our human blood there are three parts that I want to discuss, the white blood cells, the red blood cells, and the platelets. Each part has a specific function that must be performed to obtain the optimum results for our blood. Without one of the parts functioning properly the body can get weak, sick, and even die.

The white blood cells fight off infections once an infection, something foreign to us, invades our body. The red blood cells take nourishment to the body, and also collect the waste from our body and take it away. The platelets stick together when an opening is made in the body and the blood begins to flow out, thus preventing bleeding to death, or bleeding out and dying. Like most things we are discussing in this book everything is in threes, even the workings of our blood system.

The eighth day is for male circumcision, a cutting away of the flesh, a bloody portion, a bloody remnant, to be thrown away and cast aside, but mostly it signifies covenant agreement. The number 8 has significant meaning. It is the number for new beginnings. The scripture says that *"Old things are passed away; behold, all things have become new."* II Corinthians 5:17.

This 8th day represents male (and female through her later covenant) of the 'mankind' species. This takes care of the child, but the mother still has some purifying to do. She shall remain separated for thirty-three days to be purified from her loss of blood. Notice the exact days set aside are the same as the years that Jesus lived before He was crucified. Coincidence? I don't think so.

But if the child is a girl, then she shall be unclean for twice as many days, two weeks, or fourteen days. Then she shall remain separated sixty-six days to be purified, or exactly double the thirty-three days that is required for the male child. What could this mean? I know we discussed this earlier in the book but there are so many layers in the scriptures, and I want to show it to you.

It really is quite simple. Jesus is the Son of God. He is sent to the earth to take away the sins of the world. He is the ultimate sacrifice, the ultimate bloodshed, and the final sacrifice. His last words were, "It is finished."

What is finished? For one thing, all sacrifices are finished. There is no need for any others. This final one has done what all the others could not do. This final sacrifice of blood has been made to cleanse the entire Body of Christ, the entire church yet to be born. He is the perfect Lamb of God that takes away the sins of the world. This final "It is finished" sacrifice defeated Satan and all his demons and took back the keys of death and hell.   These two keys King Jesus will use when the 7 trumpets are sounded in the Book of Revelation.

What does the number 66 have to do with anything and what could it mean? Jesus is the Son of God. *"In the beginning [before all time] was the Word (Christ), and the Word was with God, and the Word was God Himself."* John 1:1 *"And the Word (Christ) became flesh (human, incarnate) and tabernacled (fixed His tent of flesh, lived awhile) among us."* John 1:14 AMPC.   The Word became flesh and dwelt among us.

It's hard to wrap our finite minds around the fact that the all powerful, all knowing, infinite eternal God, who was, is, and will be, actually clothed Himself in flesh, shed His eternal being to come to earth, bleed and die for us.   We are so undeserving; and He did it anyway.

The number 6 represents and is defined as a number for flesh or to symbolize mankind. When researching what this could mean by the 6 being multiplied by the number 11, I stopped and wept.   The number 6 represents mankind or the flesh/carnal side of mankind.   11 is the number that represents rebellion and depravity.

6 (flesh) x 11 (rebellion and depravity) = 66 (the Word of God.

When these two numbers are multiplied together, I would assume the answer would be something so horrible that humanity would not be able to even stand it. Instead the answer to carnality times rebellion and depravity is the Word of God.

There are 66 books within the Book of the Bible. Every word, and every page, every scripture revelation is the answer to mankind's carnal flesh in rebellion and depravity. The answer to man's rebellion and depravity is the Word of God.

When the Word became flesh and dwelt among us, then He, the Word, became the ultimate sacrifice. He ascended to heaven to sit at the right hand of the Father and ever intercede for us, and He didn't leave us here alone.

First, He promised that He would send a Comforter, the Holy Spirit, and in Acts 2 we see this account. But even that is not enough. We need the sacrifice with us. We need the blood on our doorposts, on our lives, as a reminder to the devil that we have been bought with a price; the ultimate sacrifice is still upon us!

"Then Moses summoned all the elders of Israel and said to them 'Go at once and select the animals for your families and slaughter the Passover lamb. Take a bunch of hyssop, dip it into the blood in the basin and put some of the blood on the top and on both sides of the doorframe. Not one of you shall go out the door of his house until morning. When the LORD goes through the land to strike down the Egyptians, He will see the blood on the top and sides of the doorframe and will pass over that doorway, and He will not permit the destroyer to enter your houses and strike you down.'" Exodus 12:21-23 NIV.

When we receive Jesus as our Lord and   Savior, He comes to

live in our hearts and will forever remain one with us. But He did something else. Just as mankind's flesh is represented by the number 6, we need to realize a very important revelation about the Hebrew language and the numbers within it. When anything in the Hebrew language is doubled it means that it is the greatest of the great. For example, we use the phrases King of kings, Lord of lords, and even the Holy of Holies.

We should realize that means there is no king higher than our King Jesus. There is no lord higher than our Lord Jesus the Christ! There is nothing more holy than the very depth of the Holy of Holies! So we should not be surprised when the Bible has taken a number that represents human flesh, 6, and by doubling it to 66, it now represents the Word having become flesh and is the greatest of all humans, Jesus Christ the Son of Man! Christ Jesus is the ultimate Man of all men. His Word represented by 66 Books washes, cleanses, and purifies humanity; the blood of the Lamb can cleanse all carnality!

The Bible, every word of it, is what comes after Jesus. When Jesus left the earth, He sent His Holy Spirit to indwell us. And He left His Word to cleanse us. Both Spirit and Truth position us as a spotless bride for the Bridegroom.

When the Word became flesh and dwelt among us, then the Word became double flesh, 66, once the ultimate sacrifice had been made, and He still dwells among us through His Spirit and His Word. The Word is continually setting us free, healing and delivering us, saving and sanctifying us, cleansing and purifying us!

Now here is the exciting part to me. The numbers that signify Jesus' life while living here on this earth represents the human male. The number 8 always represents new beginnings for all mankind. The number 7 represents the day ordained for rest when God said, *"It is finished."* Rest still holds for us today (Hebrews 4).

The number 33 represents the years that Jesus lived in the sinless flesh body and was crucified with the repetition of the words from Jesus' mouth, *"It is finished."*

Then for the female we have these numbers. The number 14 represents the separation of male and female, as completion not destruction. It is not a pulling apart of two but a choice of two becoming one. This is a double of completion, *'It is finished.'* *"For your former shame you shall receive double."* Isaiah 61:7.

Let's not forget the double anointing for Elisha who came after Elijah. Whatever comes afterward is doubled. The number 66 represents the Word of God; remember there are sixty-six books in the Bible. The Word of God is what comes out of Jesus, just as the female comes out of mankind. The Word and Jesus are One, just as the male and female are created to operate as one.

The parallels are amazing when you look at them. Instead of the female feeling like an afterthought we need to recognize the significance of our part in the earth. The female is not what is created last, but rather what is 'set apart' or separated for purification, completeness, and power of choice.

The female represents the male just as the Word of God represents the Son. In this revelation the female could never be considered 'half' or less, but 'whole' and complete. The female is in a sense, the double male, but she is also, the finished half of male. When the truth is revealed we can see that the female is the 'other sight, the other side, the other view' of mankind. This is one of the definitions in the ancient Hebrew language of the word 'helpmate.' Two parts make a whole man.

The Word of God is likened to Jesus' shadow. It is that which comes after or is left behind with the anointing in it. Woman is man's shadow, that which is left behind to complete, to finish.

She is not without power, absolutely not! Much power, the same authority, the same position, the same ability, they are not only to operate as one; in God, the male and the female ARE ONE! They are the same.

"There is neither Jew nor Gentile, neither slave nor free, nor is there male and female, for you are all one in Christ Jesus. If you belong to Christ, then you are Abraham's seed, and heirs according to the promise." Galatians 3:28-29 NIV.

In Christ we are all the same. There is no separation. We are all accepted, but we have specific purposes, callings, and positions that we are created to fill and operate, and no one can take that from us. These places, positions, and callings are for us! Anything that God does is always for our good and when we accept the perfect place designed for us, we flourish in it!

Female is the shadow, the secret place, of the male. When you think of it that makes so much sense. When the male child is circumcised on the eighth day covenant is cut between man and God. For a long time as I meditated on this I wondered in the back of my mind, "What about the female?"

My rational mind said that this eighth day, new beginnings, for all mankind was taken care of by the male child, and still is today. This covenant agreement continues on as any male child is circumcised after birth. But as I thought about this process, I just could not let it go.

I tried to reason that the male did it for the female as Christ has gone through the process of crucifixion for the Church. But there had to be more, because the scripture says that we must 'take up our cross' and follow Him. The Bible clearly states that we must go through the process of repentance and acceptance, of dying to self. These are the things that we must do as humanity to walk in covenant with God, and this is a daily process, a circle of life.

Each day another trip around the tree, each week, each month, and then each year, we are ever spiraling upward toward the goal of being birthed finally and completely into eternity. The earth experience is much like the womb experience for a fetus. It is a time of development, a process, so that once the birthing has taken place the fetus has developed into a healthy human being with what is needed physically to survive this earthly realm.

Our earthly experience is much like being in the womb. It is a process or development, maturing into the ultimate bride for Christ, without spot or wrinkle.

If the male child could actually be circumcised for the female, then what would be the importance or even the purpose for the female at all? As I thought through this process, I began to rationalize that the male is circumcised on the eighth day, then when a man and woman come together and the hymen is broken, blood is shed, and then she is 'engrafted in' so to speak to the covenant with God. But something about this just did not satisfy.

For one thing, this breaking of the hymen between a man and a woman is *their* covenant together. This is the blood that must be shed as they cut covenant together for two to become one. So where is the female's covenant agreement with God? We discussed this earlier, but I want to make sure you have the depths of the layers of the revelation.

In the book *Biblical Mathematics the number 14 is defined as 'deliverance or salvation.'   It is used 26 times in the Bible.

This book tells of how it was on the fourteenth day of the first month of the year when the children of Israel were delivered from Egyptian bondage. The number 14 is found three times connected with Christ's coming into this world and Christ's sole purpose was to save and deliver His people.

A very interesting revelation concerning the number fourteen is found in Matthew 1:17 with the generations between Abraham and Christ.

"So, all the generations from Abraham to David are fourteen generations; and from David until the carrying away into Babylon are fourteen generations, and from the carrying away into Babylon unto Christ are fourteen generations."
Matthew 1:17 KJV.

Perhaps the most interesting thought about this scripture is if you do not separate the entire generational count from Abraham to Christ into three groups the generations do not add up 14+14+14, which equals 42; but rather you actually count from Abraham to Jesus Christ and you get 40 generations! You may be thinking, "How can this be?"

Take a look at the chart below.

Abraham to David = 14 generations (Passive)
David to Babylon = 14 generations (Active)
Babylon to Jesus Christ = 14 generations (Authoritative)

To divide it out into three groups you must count the beginning and the end of each group twice. Thus giving us two generations that are counted twice when you count the entire time from Abraham to Jesus. We can subtract two from the whole total of 42, which gives us the total of 40 generations from Abraham to Jesus. This is, of course, as it should be because the number 40 means 'the end of trials, probation, and testings' according to this same book.

This makes logical sense when you look at it from the standpoint of the woman's body. It takes forty weeks for a baby to be developed from conception to birth. The children of Israel were sent into the Promised Land in Numbers 13 to spy out the promise and bring back a report. God was testing them to see if they would be led forth into the promise by their faith or by their sight.

The spies failed miserably and relied more on what they saw rather than having faith in the promise of God, so they were sent out to wander in the wilderness for another forty years.

This was not punishment but rather a time of development for their faith. Thus, God is continually teaching us how to trust Him at all times no matter what we see. God's statement throughout the Old Testament after He has judged His children time and time again is "Then they will know that I am God."

This is the statement that God is continually making to us when we come through a trial, a testing, even a probation period in our lives. "Then you will know that I am God."

So, let's go back and take a look at the number 14 for the female child. As I meditated on this for months, I finally saw the truth in this number for the feminine side of purification and most importantly, our feminine covenant with God.

In a female's natural body there is a specific time each month when a female ovulates and drops her egg of reproduction. This is her time when she is the most fertile, the most productive, to get pregnant and produce. She is definitely 'active' and ready to receive at this point each month. If she receives the gift of life through the sperm of a male, then she is impregnated, and the development of another life begins. This will take forty weeks, then a beautiful baby is born. Thus the cycle of life begins again for another human being.

If she does not receive fertilization her body waits another fourteen days and she begins her monthly period. She bleeds. Her body automatically designed by Almighty God cuts covenant with Him.

What happens during the monthly period of a female? The lining of the uterus is unproductive, so it is shed by the body and thrown off, a type of circumcision. Then the new productive skin is produced in the lining of the uterus. This bloodshed has been thought of as a curse for many generations. It is taught as a time of impurity, almost shameful. And yet, when we see it with the light of revelation, we can see the ultimate of covenant with the female and God.

When a male child is circumcised the unproductive foreskin is cut, a little blood is shed, and then that unfruitful skin is thrown away. A pruning of the flesh has taken place; covenant with God is cut and mankind has a way to the throne room of God because of the blood.

A female is not physically circumcised because the unproductive skin for her is inside of her womb. It can receive the seed and be fertile, but if this miracle does not occur, then the unproductive, unfruitful lining of the uterus is automatically shed, the blood flows and with that flow the lining is thrown off and out of the body. This prevents disease and problems later on in life and is vital for health for the female.

"Every branch in Me that does not bear fruit He takes away; and every branch that bears fruit He prunes, that it may bear more fruit. You are already clean because of the word which I have spoken to you. Abide in Me, and I in you. As the branch cannot bear fruit of itself, unless it abides in the vine, neither can you, unless you abide in Me." John 15:2-4.

Do you see the truth? Where is the female's circumcision? It is not just once in a lifetime, but as long as she is in her active stage of life every 14 days is decisive for her future and her production.   Thus, the number 14 is the number for covenant for the female.   This monthly periodic bleeding simply reminds us that God's covenant with humanity is not just a one-time thing, but it is everlasting, passing from generation to generation through the sign of the woman. The monthly bloodshed of the female is a 'covenant sign' for all mankind that God and His covenant are eternal!

We are not cursed as the female, no!   We are a sign, used as a reminder to all mankind that what God starts, He will always finish.   He continues to do what He always did generationally.   The covenant between God and mankind goes on generation to generation.   Our revelation understanding of who God is to us individually and as a sea of humanity helps us step to the third and final stage of our own lives, not always striving to prove our worth in our own strength and ability.   But when we accept the covenant made between God and mankind, both male and female, we can see the hope and everlasting union of the bride and Bridegroom, the modern-day church and Jesus Christ!

Women, you are a continual sign of the covenant agreement that God has made with mankind.   Never let yourself think again that you have been cursed just because you are a female.   Rather, you should see yourself as the Word of God, the Bible, is to Jesus, so are we to man.   We are a constant and continual reminder of God's goodness, mercy, favor, and everlasting agreement!

Chapter Twelve
God's Shadow

The huge question still remains in our minds and hearts. How did Mary, a simple little female from the region of Galilee in a tiny place called Nazareth become pregnant with the seed of the Most High God?

As the angel spoke to Mary and told her the prophetic word from above, she questioned immediately the typical question of humanity. I don't believe she questioned God's ability, or His will, or His plan. What I do believe she questioned is how this ultimate plan from heaven could be completed through her natural little limited body.

It's not that we don't think God can supply all our needs; it's that we are not capable of understanding how God can get all His riches from the region of the Spirit realm of eternity to our natural and limited realm of our lowly earthly existence.

For months and months, I have meditated on how can there

be a shadow in the secret place. How there can be a shadow in God? Remember *"He who dwells in the secret place of the Most High shall remain stable and fixed under the shadow of the Almighty [Whose power no foe can withstand]."* Psalm 91:1 AMPC.

In the King James Version it reads, *"He who dwells in the secret place of the Most High shall abide in the shadow of the Almighty."* Have you ever thought about where could the shadow of God possibly be? Has it ever occurred to you that the light source cannot cast a shadow?

I have thought about it many times. I have worked with a light source trying to get it to cast a shadow. I have never been able to make a shadow directly from the source of light. So what can this be, 'the shadow of the Almighty?'

God is light so the shadow of God must not be an actual shadow. So then, what is it? What could this and other scriptures actually be referring to, 'the shadow of the Almighty?'

God began to reveal to me several things about shadows. We were on the road several years ago and we started out the year with six weeks without a break ministering in different services all over the United States, in multiple services each week. During the first month we ministered almost every night in a different service and in a different city.

One weekend we were told of a tremendous miracle that had occurred because someone had listened to our tape on restoration. The woman did not come to the service because she had not left her home for many years. Her husband had come, and he got the tape and took it home to her. This tells you it was several decades ago as he got a 'tape.' As she listened God completely delivered this woman who had been bound for many years.

As Harry and I were discussing this, I said, "Wouldn't it have been wonderful had she been delivered like this in a service so we and others could have enjoyed this great miracle of God?"

Immediately the Lord spoke to our hearts. We heard Him say that our books and tapes are our shadow. They go where we can't go. Our shadow stretches out past where we are standing. When Peter walked among the people and his shadow fell upon them many were healed. Our ministry resources are those things we can leave behind after we have flown out of a city. When people take our books, and CDs home with them, they are taking our shadows, and the anointing of the Lord is on our shadow!

"And believers were increasingly added to the Lord, multitudes of both men and women, so that they brought the sick out into the streets and laid them on beds and couches, that at least the shadow of Peter passing by might fall on some of them. Also, a multitude gathered from the surrounding cities to Jerusalem, bringing sick people and those who were tormented by unclean spirits, and they were all healed." Acts 5:14-16.

Was there power in Peter's shadow in Acts 5? How could there have been? As we meditated on this it became clear that God is not talking about a literal shadow that is cast when an object stands in front of the light source. This shadow is referring to the anointing. Of course, it might have been Peter's actual shadow, but it was the anointing of God that was present to heal in Peter's life; even his shadow was anointed.

I believe my shadow carries the anointing of the Lord. I believe every note I sing, every word I say, every time I pray, God's anointing is there. Even when you read these words in this book, my shadow, the very anointing in my life is in every word. The anointing is here to heal you and set you free, deliver you from anything the devil has tried to steal, kill, and destroy; the anointing is here for you!

God cannot cast a shadow because in heaven there is no shadow of turning according to the Word of God. In Psalm 91 the shadow is the anointing of God, like the glory cloud. Clouds cast a 'shadow' onto the ground below.

The anointing of God is the shadow. *"I shall abide in the shadow of the Almighty"* is referring to living, abiding, and dwelling in the anointing of Almighty God! God is telling us that if we are willing, we can literally live, dwell, and have our permanent residence in the anointing of God!

When Peter walked among the people it was the anointing of God that fell on people as he walked by that caused them to be healed. It is the anointing of God on our ministry resources, every word in every book, and every note on every worship CD, that can cause people to be set free and healed as they read and listen. The anointing of God is not subject to time or space. It matters not how long ago the books were written or the words were spoken or sung on the cds.

I have read books of many great heroes in the faith. When I read the words that were written many years ago the anointing of God is still on the words, as it was on their lives. We have to think 'out of the box' to understand this, but our lives will continue to do what we do now, even after we have left this earth and we continue to live in eternity if we are anointed. If Jesus tarries and we go to heaven before the coming of the Lord, what we do now will affect many people much later! The anointing of God is forever! And we have been given the invitation to move in and live there with God! With this invitation comes the authority and ability to do it, despite our circumstances.

Chapter Thirteen
God Revealed

"In the beginning God."

I heard the Lord say, "I was there."

Then God said, "You were there."

As I finish this book, I want to share with you this little statement.   Father God loves to 'blow our natural minds.' He does it to me regularly when I walk with Him and talk with Him. When I slow down my natural busy-ness and stop my doing, He shows me. He talks to me.

I think He laughs sometimes. In fact, I hear Him laugh out loud sometimes when He shows me things. His laughter melts away all the cares of this world in an instant.

God said to me, "That's right. In the beginning everything that ever was, is, and will be, was, is, and will be in Me." I saw it. I can't explain it or even write it, but I saw it. Before time began as we know it I saw it. God is. I saw Him. I couldn't get my mind around it, but I saw Him, not fully, but a dimension of Him. He is ONE, COMPLETE, WHOLE, UNITY, ALL.

God said to me, "You live on a horizontal timeline, with an arrow at each end of time, and you are only able to imagine this dimension. But I am showing you that I AM in all places, time, and space at the same time and dimension." God said, "Time IS in Me. Time is vertical, horizontal, a prism dimension, in every direction and at every degree. When you finally 'see' all of the directions and dimensions, then there are trillionth times trillionth more directions and dimensions to see. In Me, everything is and always will be, never ending in every direction and dimension."

Words can never show you this dimension of time. I pray that God gives every reader the same vision that He showed me of Himself, just so you can begin to fathom the depth and height and magnitude of our God. God showed me how He IS in the beginning, the middle, and the end all at the same time.

He showed me that this is how He predestines situations and people. Not that He ever chooses for us, but He foreknows what we will choose before we ever actually get there in our finite dimension.

He foreknows because He IS THERE AHEAD OF OUR TIME WITH US WHEN WE CHOOSE! Try and wrap your mind around that! Because He is and He will be at the same time God is with you in your future before you are ever there. He knows what you will choose because He was with us when we chose in our future!

When you are in the dimension of the spirit you don't actually have to speak, you just think, and it's as if you have spoken! I thought,"Why was there ever anything other than 'In the beginning God?' Why would there have ever needed to be anything other than this?"

Oneness, unity, are words that Harry and I have been studying and meditating on and attempting to live ever since God called us out of our two separate ministries and told us to operate and minister as 'one' in one ministry.

"In the beginning God, seems to be the perfect oneness," I thought. God said to me, "Everything that is, was, and will be was in Me in the beginning, including Lucifer, humanity, time, space, matter, EVERYTHING." I am ONE because I AM ONE. I AM ONE by design. I want to be "One with you" by choice. Not My choice but all of humanities' choice to choose to be one with Me. Everyone and everything were one in ME not by choice but by design. Everyone and everything were perfect and anointed until they weren't anymore. There was the moment when iniquity was found in Lucifer. He had his until moment."

All of a sudden, I realized the heartbreak of our Father God. I began to see the PURE-I-FIRE that raged and had to purge the choice of sin over the choice of holy oneness with Almighty God. I was suddenly afraid and unsettled at the realization of this scene.

I began to get a glimpse of the dimension God was showing me by the Spirit. It shook my religious mind to the core. God wants me to choose to love Him, serve Him, and be One with Him; He wants that to be My choice. Not because I am in Him, but because I choose to be IN HIM.

In our simple language I related it like this. God didn't want an arranged marriage between the divine Bridegroom and His eternal bride, with no choice involved. He wants us to choose to 'die to self' and become 'one' with Him. He wants us to choose to be His bride by our own decision, our own choice. He doesn't want us by divine design; He wants us by our own choice.

My mind was racing because this made so much sense, and it made other things make so much sense. This is why male and female must choose to operate as one and become one. God takes two and by our own choices He then allows us to become 'one flesh' in marriage. Not just one flesh, but one soul, and one spirit while we are here in this earth realm, and if oneness is attained here then it will last for eternity.

This would solve so many questions that we hear from husbands and wives. Will we be married in heaven? Will he still be my husband? Will she still be my wife? Sometimes these questions are asked out of hearts that cannot imagine spending eternity apart or separated from their beloved mates. Other times the questions are asked because they cannot wait to be 'free' from the other person and heaven seems to be their only hope of release. From what I have seen and experienced from this vision I would say that the one that cannot imagine being apart is the couple that has truly become 'one' here on the earth and will remain one through eternity.

You may have known couples like this, though probably not many. These are the ones who have no way of knowing how to live on this earth when their mate has gone on to heaven ahead of them. I knew a couple like this, my grandparents.

My dad's mom and dad were very spiritual. They were on a different level than most people. They didn't have the revelation that we have today because I venture to say that much of what we see now was not revealed to the earth, or at least to them, at that time. But with what they did have in the spirit, they walked in it.   As long as I can remember they were hardly ever sick and never with anything seriously wrong with them.

When I was fifteen years old my grandfather began to show signs of skin cancer. He was progressively worse over the next few months. While he was getting closer and closer to heaven each week, my grandmother began to have signs of congestive heart failure in her body.

This all happened over a few short months. They died two weeks apart with two totally unrelated illnesses in which neither had signs of before! They were 'one' here and could not seem to live without the other. You may have heard of similar events in other marriages.

Then there are the other married people who cannot wait to be 'free' from each other in heaven. Those people have never been 'one' here, but have only been legally married by human definition, not God's definition of marriage. God has given us the opportunity to live and walk as 'one' in marriage. Accepting anything less than this is denying God the authority that He has predestined for us on the earth.

In closing, I want to go back and neatly tie a bow around the revelation of the finished and final stage for Mary as she completed her divine destiny. She spoke to the servants in John 2 to do whatever He says. She was in her final stage of life. She had her authority. She knew it was time. She knew it had to be at the wedding. She knew in the last days the bride would understand.

As these words came from her mouth to the servants, she was telling her Son that she released Him to be and do what He was created to be and do. Whether she ever spoke these words or not, I believe Jesus heard her.

I believe Mary said to her Son as He was transitioning into His next stage of life, "Jesus, God gave You to me for such a time as this. I release You into Your ministry, Your life's mission. I release You as Your mother, to step out into Your calling. You are no longer my Son, but You are now my Messiah. Do what You have to do; complete the task. I will walk You as far as I can on this side, and then wait for me on the other side. I will come when God allows me as I finish my destiny." She didn't just release Him into His ministry. She released Him to be the Lamb of God. She pushed Him to the cross.

These were the same words that I told Gabrielle when she crossed over on the third day after I released her. It is not by accident that Gabrielle died on a Tuesday, the third day, the bride's day. Harry and I told her we would walk her as far on this side as we were allowed to go. Then we would stay here until God calls us over. I told her to wait for me; that I was coming. My plan was to cross over quickly, but God had other plans. He told me to stay here until He called me and do the work that He has assigned me to do. I'm still here. I'm still waiting.

Part of that assignment was to get this revelation in print for you to read. It has taken me over twenty years to finish this book. The revelation has come in layers and with time. I know that it is a book for this season, a revelation for this time on the earth. I know it is for His bride. It is for such a time as this.

We must learn to move forward, progress, through this life experience. We must learn to stop hanging up on the details, and distractions of this present world. We must learn to listen and obey the voice of the Master, Father.

What stage of life are you now? Are you progressing or are you stuck? What is stopping you from transitioning to the next stage of life?   Physically, the three levels move at their own pace and we can do very little to change the progressions.   Emotionally, we must go through the processes of time, troubles, trials, to grow and mature into the emotional health and well being that we are called to be. Spiritually, we move through these three levels also.   Ever progressing toward the third and final stage where we can proclaim as Mary did, "They have no more wine.   No more blood!"

With the understanding of the scriptures that I have painstakingly laid out for you, I pray you can receive the plan of God that He has for you to finish your life's journey strong.   You were created to finish strong. not crawl across the finish line. You are a finisher and have the anointing of a finisher. Jesus is the author and finisher!! We are finishers in Him! We can proclaim together, "No more blood! I am ready to move to the final authoritative stage of my spiritual life. I trust You totally and completely.   I give up needing control of my life, my future, and my circumstances.   I rest inside Your presense.   I hide myself in Your bosom, as I lay my head on Your chest. I know that I can relax and enjoy the ride of the Spirit with You, my Strength and my Redeemer."

About the Author

Cheryl Salem walked the runway to become Miss America 1980, despite what appeared to be all odds stacked against her. A horrific car crash resulting in a physical handicap and over 100 stitches in her face, were no match for what God had planned for her life. Through childlike faith in Him, she overcame the obstacles and eventually took the crown in Atlantic City to become Miss America 1980. She has used this distinction as a springboard to launch the gospel into churches, women's conferences, and many television appearances. According to Cheryl, "None of these things would be possible, if not for my Jesus."

In 1985, Cheryl married the love of her life, Harry Salem II. Harry and Cheryl Salem travel the world ministering the gospel, telling people that Jesus loves them and that He is returning soon! Their lives revolve around seeking the Lord and where He would have them go. Two by two they travel, loving God's people, living and moving in His anointing.

In 1999, Harry and Cheryl endured the loss of their 6-year-old daughter, Gabrielle. As they boldly took steps of faith to overcome the agonizing pain of Gabrielle's death, they asked God to restore them and for souls to come into His kingdom. God has restored the Salem family and because of His mighty anointing, the altars have been full!

Harry and Cheryl are committed to leading godly lives as an example to their sons, Harry III and Roman. Harry and Cheryl are blessed to have their entire family in ministry with them. Harry III continues in the family ministry as well as Roman and his beautiful wife, Stephanie, their daughter-in-love. Healing and restoration have come full circle to the Salem family with the miracle births of Mia Gabrielle and Roman Harry.

Cheryl and Harry have written 39 books. From her first book *A Bright Shining Place* to one of her latest, ***Women Of The Nation, Pray!*** her books are open and honest with such transparency you can almost hear her talking to you while you read! She has recorded numerous worship music projects, from prophetic books of the Bible, lullabies, instrumentals, prophetic flowing intercession, and beautiful worship CDs. Her latest worship CD, *Enter In* is her most anointed project so far!

Cheryl is founder and president of **Women Of The Nation**, an organization that is bringing together thousands of women who stand, pray and believe for this country. Under Cheryl's leadership these women are strategic, organized, unified and in prayer battle for this nation. **Women Of The Nation** Summits are held from coast to coast. God gave Cheryl authority when she was crowned Miss America and she is using that authority to stand in the gap for this great nation, for such a time as this!

Other books by Salem Family Ministries

Women of the Nation Pray!

I Am A Worshiper

I Am A Worshiper Workbook

We Who Worship

We Who Worship Workbook

Rebuilding the Ruins of Worship

Rebuilding the Ruins of Worship Workbook

Tones of the Throne Room

Tones of the Throne Room Workbook

The Rise of an Orphan Generation: Longing for a Father

Two Becoming One

Don't Kill Each Other! Let God Do It!

From Mourning to Morning

From Grief to Glory

Distractions from Destiny

Obtaining Peace – A 40-Day Prayer Journal

Entering Rest – Be Still – A 40-Day Journey into the Presence of God

The Presence of Angels in Your Life

Overcoming Fear – A 40-Day Prayer Journal

A Bright Shining Place - The Story of a Miracle

Speak the Word Over Your Family for Finances

Speak the Word Over Your Family for Healing

Speak the Word Over Your Family for Salvation

The Choice is Yours

Being #1 at Being #2 (out of print)

Every Body needs Balance

For Men Only

A Royal Child

The Mommy Book

Abuse ... Bruised but not Broken

You Are Somebody

Choose to be Happy (out of print)

Health and Beauty Secrets (out of print)

Simple Facts: Salvation, Healing & the Holy Ghost (out of print)

* *Grave Raiders*

* *Feminine Spirits and Angels*

* *Investigating Wonders*

* *The Sound of the Spirit*

* *Age of Mystery*

* *Counting Ten Fingers for Patience* Children's Book

* *Ten Shots for Do and Don't* Children's Book

* *Ten Steps to Build and Be Spirit Filled* Children's Book

* *Count of Ten Say Amen* Children's Book

* * Written by Dr. Harry Salem III

EBooks available at salemfamilyministries.org

Worship CDs and downloads are also available

If you would like more information about Salem Family Ministries, you can write to us or contact us via email on our website.

Salem Family Ministries
P. O. Box 1595
Cathedral City, CA 92235
www.salemfamilyministries.org

https://www.facebook.com/Salemfamilyministries.org/

Subscribe to our YouTube channel Salem Family Ministries and follow us daily at 9:00 AM PST as we journey through the Bible, one book at a time, one chapter a day.

Marriage Monday Nights 6:00 PM PST

Thrive Thursday Nights Prayer 6:00 PM PST

Follow me on instagram, CherylSalem1957

Made in the USA
Monee, IL
16 March 2021